Reach out...
Become an
Encourager

Reach out...
Become an Encourager

Stanley E. Lindquist, Ph.D.
Founder and President • Link Care Foundation

Illustrations by Phil Brewer

Creation House • Wheaton, Illinois

Published by Creation House, 396 E. St. Charles Rd., Wheaton, Illinois 60188

All Biblical quotations from the King James Version.

ISBN 0-88419-188-5
Library of Congress Catalog No. 83-70388
Printed in the United States of America.

Creation House is a ministry of Christian Life Missions. Its purpose is to publish and distribute Bibles, books and other Christian literature presenting the gospel of Jesus Christ. If you would like additional information, we encourage you to write to us at 396 E. St. Charles Rd., in Wheaton, IL 60188.

Dedication

I dedicate this book to all those who have
been of help to others through the Link Care
Foundation: the Board, the Staff, Missionaries
and clients, all who have sharpened my awareness.

CONTENTS

PREFACE

This book comes from my recognition, over the years, of some basic, helpful principles common to all effective, encouraging relationships. In one form or another, these principles were employed by Christ himself. Just enough is revealed in the Scriptures to whet the appetite of those who are eager to translate the somewhat indefinable and invisible love of God within them into words and actions that others can understand and embrace.

No experience is more frustrating than wanting to help another know the love of God that we have experienced, yet being rebuffed because our words or motives are misunderstood. This book, with its emphasis on applying practical principles of interpersonal relations, can help you learn to translate your positive, helpful intentions into behaviors and words that will effectively communicate God's love to others.

However, interpersonal skills alone are not enough for effective encouragement. The average person needing help needs most of all to develop specific techniques for meeting the problems that he faces within and without. He needs to learn new, productive habits to replace the maladaptive ones that have such a grip on him and prevent him from being the person he wants to be. True encouragement means helping another to gain insight into his problems and to make the changes he needs to make.

I believe that the Spirit of God can minister to others through people like you who are trained in helping others develop interpersonal skills and problem-solving techniques. If you know how to use and teach those skills, you will be able to give effective encouragement to those who need it.

Much of the work done to achieve a good interpersonal relationship is supracultural. After all, a human is a human first and he adds his culture to the basic needs and emotions he starts with. These principles of relating to others are above all, supracultural, and with proper adjustment can be applied to any person in any culture as long as each of us is aware of the cultural effects on personality.

As my book *Action Helping Skills*, a book about encouragement, went out of print, someone suggested to me that it be revised and republished. Rather than simply making a few changes and calling it a revised edition, I decided to rewrite the entire book, condensing it and using case histories to illustrate the general principles being taught. The result is this new book. It comes to you with my hope that it will help you to become more effective in your encouragement to others and that a cadre of paraprofessionals can be trained to become an effective adjunct to the work of the church.

Some years ago, I lectured at Fuller Seminary for Dr. Bob Munger's class for new preachers. My idea that dedicated laymen could be a primary referral source for pastors was enthusiastically accepted by the students. Since then, it has met with similar enthusiasm from pastors who are open to new ways to enhance their ministry. As more and more laymen become effective in applying Jesus' principles and current psychological understandings of developing relationships, the work of the church can be expanded.

"All truth is God's truth." That applies to the truths of psychology as well as other truths. We in the church have not made as adequate an application of the insights of psychology as we might, partly because of artificial barriers erected by those who feel that psychology is a tool of Satan. On the other side, a fear of psychology has sometimes been fostered by professionals who are afraid they will lose business if people in the church become too active in counseling. They want to maintain a "mystique" based on fear of the unknown, much as the ancient medicine man did.

The principles and truths of psychology can be used by the Spirit of God to minister to any of God's people. I personally have been using the insights of psychology for more than 30 years of ministry. The Link Care Foundation employs psychological as well as spiritual principles in working with hundreds of missionary candidates, missionaries, and other Christians, with positive results.

Anyone can have a healing, therapeutic ministry if he is open to others, willing to listen, and ready to learn new ways to be an effective encourager. My thanks to the many clients and students who have taught me much of the information I am sharing in this book. Without them, this book would not have been written. In addition, I feel an increasing indebtedness to all those who, through lecture and literature, have taught me the principles presented here. Beverly Burch was most helpful in this revision, as Kathie Faverty was in my first endeavor. Also Phil Brewer's illustrations helped a lot. Perhaps most of all, I appreciate those significant persons in my life—my family and my close friends—whose reading and criticism have stimulated me in my work. Especially am I grateful to God and for that faith that has played such a significant part in integrating my life, impelling me to move on to new endeavors.

Stanley E. Lindquist, Ph.D.
Fresno, California, 1982

INTRODUCTION

"I really like talking to him. I always feel encouraged, no matter how difficult things are. He helps me accept and understand my feelings. He encourages me to analyze my problems and figure out what to do. He doesn't give me a lot of advice I can't or won't use—or sympathize—or agree with everything I say.

"His kind of encouragement lasts, and that's what I need—not drippy sentimentality, the 'go pray about it' kind of stuff I so often get. I know I need to pray, and I have been praying a lot, so I don't like to have someone imply that I haven't prayed. He helps me put feet on my prayers. *That's encouraging!*"

Would you like to be described that way?

You can.

But—it takes work.

Will you do it?

If you are willing to try, you already have made the first step toward becoming an Encourager—a facilitator, a peer counselor, a paraprofessional helper.

It's up to *you*!

Being an effective encourager does not come naturally. Perhaps you already have some helpful qualities, so people often come to you with their problems. That's good—but do you really help? Are you more than a listener? Do you help the seekers of encouragement to learn to *help themselves*? Or do you—

- give advice (rather than helping them take responsibility for themselves)?
- sympathize (rather than developing empathy)?
- judge and condemn (rather than helping them to evaluate themselves)?

Those are traps an encourager must learn to avoid.

Paul was often an encourager, but once he made what some might think was a real mistake. His companion Mark had failed him in the midst of a missionary journey; he had gotten tired or homesick and had gone home. Then, when he wanted to go on the next journey, Paul was not an encourager; he said, "*No!*"

But Barnabas said, "*Yes.*"

And so Paul and Barnabas argued. Paul was firm and Barnabas was firm—so they parted company. Paul took Silas; Barnabas took Mark; and they had two teams instead of one (Acts 15:36-41). Barnabas was the encourager. If someone had failed once, must he be forever branded a failure?

The result of Barnabas' encouragement is evident today, for we read the book Mark wrote, one of the Gospels. Maybe it would not have been written—or at least not by Mark—without Barnabas' encouragement.

We'd all like to be like Paul. Perhaps we'd better be like Barnabas, the encourager, instead. Encouragers usually work in the background. But often their work is much appreciated by others. It always is honored by God, who sees secret things and rewards them openly.

Jesus' relationships with others, described in the Gospels,

give us a model for encouragement. He first developed the kind of rapport in which it was possible to communicate openly because trust, caring, and love were apparent. In most cases Jesus' reputation had helped pave the way for that rapport. When people come to a person for help and understanding, they already have placed confidence in that person and are ready to listen to him.

Most of the contacts you and I make do not have the prior preparation that Jesus' contacts had, so we have to do more to develop the kind of rapport that Jesus quickly established. However, as we learn and practice relationship-building skills, the ability to develop encouraging relationships grows and becomes more natural. A change occurs almost without our being aware of it—but others are, and so they come to be encouraged.

We must overcome many barriers in meeting and speaking to others if we are to relate, communicate, encourage, and help. One of the most striking scriptural illustrations of Jesus' overcoming barriers to communication is his conversation with a woman at a well in Samaria (John 4:4-39). Not only was this woman blocked by prejudices because she was a Samaritan and female, but presumably she had been ostracized in her town because of her immorality.

In spite of those barriers, Jesus attended physically, psychologically, perceptually, and spiritually to that woman. He responded to her needs and accepted her self-disclosures. Further, he encouraged her to do something as a result of his communication with her.

The woman, in turn, responded to Jesus. She opened herself to new ideas, listened, and started on a course of action that had far-reaching effects, not only in her own life but also in the lives of others. That rejected woman changed in a way that was visible, and those who before had snubbed her now not only listened to her but followed her suggestion, "Come and see this man." They came out in the heat of the

day to listen to Christ because she had been encouraged and
had become, herself, an encourager.

Jesus left Judea and departed again into Galilee. And he
must needs go through Samaria. Then cometh he to a city of
Samaria, which is called Sychar, near to the parcel of ground
that Jacob gave to his son Joseph. Now Jacob's well was there.
Jesus therefore, being wearied with his journey, sat thus on
the well: and it was about the sixth hour. There cometh a
woman of Samaria to draw water: Jesus saith unto her, Give
me to drink. (For his disciples were gone away unto the city
to buy meat.) Then saith the woman of Samaria unto him,
How is it that thou, being a Jew, askest drink of me, which
am a woman of Samaria? for the Jews have no dealings with
the Samaritans. Jesus answered and said unto her, If thou
knewest the gift of God, and who it is that saith to thee, Give
me to drink; thou wouldest have asked of him, and he would
have given thee living water. The woman saith unto him, Sir,
thou hast nothing to draw with, and the well is deep: from
whence then hast thou that living water? Art thou greater
than our father Jacob, which gave us the well, and drank
thereof himself, and his children, and his cattle? Jesus answered and said unto her, Whosoever drinketh of this water
shall thirst again: but whosoever drinketh of the water that I
shall give him shall never thirst; but the water that I shall
give him shall be in him a well of water springing up into
everlasting life. The woman saith unto him, Sir, give me this
water, that I thirst not, neither come hither to draw. Jesus
saith unto her, Go, call thy husband, and come hither. The
woman answered and said, I have no husband. Jesus said
unto her, Thou hast well said, I have no husband: for thou
hast had five husbands; and he whom thou now hast is not
thy husband: in that saidst thou truly. The woman saith unto
him, Sir, I perceive that thou art a prophet. Our fathers wor-
shipped in this mountain; and ye say, that in Jerusalem is the
place where men ought to worship. Jesus saith unto her,
Woman, believe me, the hour cometh, when ye shall neither
in this mountain, nor yet at Jerusalem, worship the Father. Ye

worship ye know not what: we know what we worship: for
salvation is of the Jews. But the hour cometh, and now is,
when the true worshippers shall worship the Father in spirit
and in truth: for the Father seeketh such to worship him.
God is a Spirit: and they that worship him must worship him
in spirit and in truth. The woman saith unto him, I know
that Messias cometh, which is called Christ: when he is come,
he will tell us all things. Jesus saith unto her, I that speak
unto thee am he. . . . The woman then left her waterpot, and
went her way into the city, and saith to the men, Come, see a
man, which told me all things that ever I did: is not this the
Christ? Then they went out of the city, and came unto
him. . . . And many of the Samaritans of that city believed
on him for the saying of the woman, which testified, He told
me all that ever I did (John 4:4-26, 28-30, 39).

"But," you say, "that was Jesus. He had powers beyond
mine. He could see things that I cannot see. He could encourage because he knew and understood in ways I cannot.
He could initiate action in the life of another. Jesus, as God,
is capable in ways that I am not."

True, Jesus was God; but he was also man. His divinity
need not discourage us. Jesus' example *as a man* demonstrates methods all of us can develop and follow. And each
Christian has God living within to aid him in his efforts to
encourage. Each of us can learn to attend to others as Jesus
did and to communicate, both verbally and nonverbally, that
we are listening. We can learn to accept others genuinely
even though our differences seem great. We can learn to respond to others' behavior, feelings, and ideas. As we learn
more about another, we can learn to understand him and
help him understand himself more fully. When we have dis-
solved the barriers, we can encourage that special, seeking
person we are communicating with either to achieve the
goals he desires or to recognize the inappropriateness of his
goals and the need to find new ones.

This book is designed to help you learn (1) to respond to another person's experiences so that he knows that you understand him; (2) to nurture that budding relationship so that you grow together; and (3) to help another change maladaptive behaviors to productive ones consistent with an experience of God's love. When you help another both to understand himself and to act on his understanding, you are following Jesus' pattern and can be called an *encourager!*

The material is divided into a series of steps, each broken down into simple increments that can be learned and practiced until they become a spontaneous, natural part of your relating to others. As you learn and use these principles, the Spirit of God will add his dynamic power to each interchange.

The following terms will be used in this book:

Facilitator: You—who respond to another person and help him learn how to become self-directing in getting along with others and in solving problems. This is another name for *encourager.*

Seeker: The one who comes to you for companionship, for encouragement, to disclose needs, and to learn with you the skills for meeting those needs.

In a sense, we all are seekers. You are seeking to learn the skills of encouragement and help to others. As you learn the skills of facilitating, you will find that your seeker will teach you, too, how to be more effective in dealing with your own problems. You will grow as your friend grows.

It is hoped that this book will open doors of understanding for you and that you go on to learn more than is presented here. Each relationship you build with another person should become a stimulus goading you to learn more.

If you are serious about increasing your encouraging skills, the practical exercises included in chapters 2-7 will help you to do so. There is no substitute for putting into action what you learn.

I pray that the Spirit of God will encourage you as you read, study, contemplate, review, and apply the relationship principles we can draw from the teaching and life of Jesus, the great Encourager.

1

You Can Begin Encouraging Today

"Today, when I got the newspaper, I saw on the front page a picture of a boy I had tried so hard to help but couldn't. Yesterday he killed a man."

Margaret, a student in our helping-skills training class, broke down sobbing, unable to continue. Finally she spoke again and began telling us how she had tried to help the boy. She had gone far beyond the second mile in her encouragement. She had visited his home, had invited him to her own home, had bought him things he needed. Now her help seemed as if it had been for naught.

Then she made a statement I will always remember: *"The hardest thing to bear is that I believe that if I had known then what I know now about helping, I could have reached him.* My experience with the other students, the books I've read in this class, our class discussions, the lectures, and the practice we've had in learning how to dissolve barriers and encourage—they could have made the difference. If I had only known—."

She broke down again. We were all moved by her sad experience; there was not a dry eye in the room. But perhaps our tears were also for ourselves, for the opportunities we might have missed for reaching those who had come to us for encouragement and help, or for those whom we hadn't even realized needed our help. We searched our souls as she was searching hers.

Are you in the same place? Is anyone reaching out to you for help? Do you know how to encourage?

Margaret began the most important lesson in becoming an encourager: she began learning about herself. She learned that she had areas of her personality that needed to be changed and improved. She recognized her need to learn specific helping skills. She used that awareness to grow.

Openness to learning is essential to becoming an encourager. And little learning takes place without awareness of one's areas of weakness or difficulty. So the first step in learning to encourage is to be open to ourselves and aware of how we feel. Having "listened" to ourselves, we can then attend and listen carefully to another, which allows him to reveal himself.

The following case encapsulates the principles and skills presented in this book. It will give you an overview of what you are about to learn.

When Milt came to the office, I could tell by the tension in his face that he was deeply distressed. Even coming to my office was very upsetting to a man who believed he should be able to master everything on his own and not rely on anyone else for help. To be in my office was a confession of inadequacy. But his need for help had overridden his need to feel self-sufficient.

Sitting down, Milt tried to speak, but nothing would come out at first. Then he mumbled a few words about trivial matters. He started again to tell me his problem, but still couldn't bring himself to do it. He paused. He sighed. He

The barrier was hard and strong

fidgeted. He was the picture of discomfort, and tension seemed to permeate the air. I felt myself almost being dragged into the bog of distrust, but I resisted and waited for the change that I knew would come if I were patient and conveyed my openness to Milt.

Finally he said, "I'm so anxious, I wonder if I'm going to lose my mind! I'm afraid I'm going crazy. I don't trust anyone. I don't trust you—even though I've been told that you are dependable and won't ever reveal what I say.

"I just can't bring myself to tell you what's bothering me, so how can you help me? I just can't. I can't!"

With that, Milt started to cry. He tried to hide the tears, but they rolled down his cheeks, and sobs racked his body. He was so upset, it was difficult for me not to interfere in his struggle.

I don't trust anyone

Moments like that are like the birth of a butterfly. If someone were to interfere with the insect as it struggles to break out of its cocoon, its full development would never take place. Similarly, if I had interfered with Milt's struggle, I would have jeopardized the potential helpfulness of our relationship.

Milt's sobs finally subsided. I reassured him that even strong men cry—something he already knew, but in moments like that, even the obvious bears repetition. At that point, the encouragement Milt needed was not mushy sentimentality but a sincere recognition of his problems, allowing him to disclose them freely.

Even though Milt knew everything he said was confidential, he still needed to be reassured many times that no one else would know his story. His guard was up. He had never before told anyone about his struggles. His thoughts seemed so black, he was sure that no one could hear them and still have any respect for him. If anyone else ever knew, it would seem like the end of life itself.

The barriers Milt had erected against sharing what were to him weird and horrible thoughts—his "macho" self-sufficiency and his fear of coming for help—are common, and they are difficult to dissolve or circumvent. The first task for anyone hoping to help another is to remove the roadblocks to openness and free communication. This must be done carefully so as not to set up a pattern in which the seeker abdicates to the helper his own responsibility for disclosing and, eventually, solving his problems. It takes time, reassurance, and a permissive atmosphere for the seeker to gain the confidence he needs for self-disclosure.

Lest you lose heart at this difficult beginning stage, remember: the person seeking help *has come to you.* He has opened himself at least that much. Therefore, he has some sense that you are trustworthy. His coming is nonverbal acceptance of you. *Build on that important aspect of your initial relationship.* Don't let it slip away from you. Be encouraging and helpful. Don't convey shock or discomfort with what he tells you. Avoid any evidence of being judgmental. Any indication of those attitutes will slam the door on your potential usefulness in encouraging him.

Milt finally began to talk a little about his problems. What he started with was not particularly unusual, and he knew it. Sharing something "safe" helped him to gain confidence in himself and in me. He was testing both me and the counseling situation.

Milt had had many problems growing up. An absentee father had hindered him in developing good relationships with men. Because of that lack, he had always felt inadequate. On the other hand, he had been too attached to his mother. His life had not been what it should have, and because it had not been right—or at least had not felt right—none of his present relationships seemed right, either.

The theme of wrongness pervaded Milt's thoughts. His negative feelings became a funnel into which he poured his thoughts about most of his experiences, which confirmed his sense of inadequacy and helplessness. Each new incident or idea triggered the mechanical recycling of negative thoughts, and he was so consumed by the buzzing confusion that he was worn out. He couldn't go on. It was too hard. Reality seemed to be slipping away. Forgetfulness and inattention began to interfere with his work—the only thing that gave him any hope and positive direction. His wife couldn't comprehend what was happening.

But still Milt balked at sharing his problem. *I'm not sure. Is this really going to be totally confidential? Can I risk exposing myself?*

Early in any relationship is a period of testing. None of us wants to expose himself to someone who will treat his confidences carelessly or minimize his feelings. Therefore, your seeker will try you out to see what you will do with his confidences.

If you pass that first test by accepting and maintaining confidentiality in even semiprivate matters, your seeker will feel free to go on. If you don't communicate acceptance and concern, you will confirm his suspicion that no one really cares. Any further revelation will seem risky and foolish to him, and he will pull back into himself.

Your first contact with a seeker is crucial. You must consciously plan your responses. At the same time, you must be warm, accepting, and spontaneous. (Though those two dictums seem contradictory, they are not if you have completely internalized the skills of encouragement.) How you handle the testing-out stage will determine the progress of your relationship.

A key way to help another person know you are really accepting him is to reflect—echo back or paraphrase—what he has said. When a person hears what he has just said from another, he knows that the other has really listened to him, understood him, and he will want to go further in talking to you and helping you to understand him.

As I used this technique of reflection, Milt became more comfortable in talking with me. He had tested me and had decided that I would not let him down, so he revealed a little more. It was hard. Seldom had I seen a person struggle so much or require so much reassurance.

When he told about some of his, until now, hidden thoughts, he again broke down. He had been struggling with those thoughts for years, never daring to tell anyone about them. He was so ashamed!

As I accepted each revelation, he began to realize that his thoughts were not as strange as he had believed. He explained more of the background of his fears and anxiety and the reasons for the difficulties he had in dealing with them. As he talked, all of his pent-up emotions began to surface. From time to time he was racked with sobs and groans. He wondered aloud, "How could any man have so much to reveal? How can I ever cope with these problems? Will this talking really help?"

Nonjudgmental acceptance is crucial to helping someone open up to you. The second he senses that you are holding what he says against him, he will not reveal any more. Why should he? To tell you more would add more damaging evidence!

A person in need of help doesn't need condemnation. He is already an expert in self-condemnation. He has spent hours, days, weeks and even years condemning himself, just as Milt had been doing. Self-condemning thoughts are circu-

Self-condemnation

lar, spiraling higher and higher with each repetition, until the person is almost driven mad. Breaking the spiral of circular thinking can start with the recognition that another human being has accepted one's thoughts without condemnation.

You may fear that by accepting negative thoughts you are endorsing them, giving them your seal of approval. Later, we will discuss that issue in more detail. For now, be assured that a person who feels as Milt did would not be likely to interpret your acceptance as approval. He already condemns himself far more than you can imagine. As a result, when he realizes that you accept him, he won't immediately assume that he is all right the way he is. The reason he is revealing his horrible thoughts is that he wants to change. When you accept him as he is, he can begin to build on that acceptance and come to recognize God's forgiveness and help in restoration and growth.

As Milt felt accepted, he struggled to clarify what he was saying. He wanted me to know exactly how he felt. He wanted to purge himself of the evil thoughts that were plaguing him. He desperately wanted to explain how he had come to be trapped by them.

Periodically he still had misgivings about revealing himself to me. Yet, because he felt accepted, he also wanted to be understood. He hadn't helped himself by keeping his disturbing thoughts to himself. Revealing them to another person at least was a step toward help. So Milt kept revealing more, attempting to clarify his ideas to me, and as he did so, he began to gain a clearer understanding of himself.

Helping another person understand himself is impossible unless he feels accepted by you. When your seeker feels accepted he will want to be understood and will try one approach after another to make things clearer to you.

An important corollary is that a person won't want to understand himself unless he accepts himself. If he is angry or dissatisfied with himself or feels inadequate and worthless, he will try to avoid revealing himself. You, as his encourager, can help him to begin to accept himself as you accept him. Your acceptance of him will facilitate his willingness to ac-

Forgiving yourself after being forgiven

cept himself. As a result, he will gain the security to reveal more about himself, even negative or upsetting things.

Understanding and clarification work both ways. The seeker *clarifies his own view of himself* as he clarifies himself to you. You are not selfishly gathering information for yourself; you are helping your seeker to understand himself, too, even if all you do is repeat to him what he says. Often my clients will say, "I have never understood things that way before!" This new insight, when we had only been covering what seemed to be old information, is often as surprising to me as it is to them.

Milt began to understand himself better as he talked. His self-perception began to grow. There was a growing awareness not only of *why* he felt the way he did but also that he could *do* something about his feelings. He no longer saw himself as a helpless pawn of each thought or incident that occurred. When someone said something derogatory, he no longer needed to be driven into the dumps. He could consider the source and evaluate what was said. If it was accurate, he could change. If it was not, he could dismiss it.

Milt's self-perception subtly changed as he recognized that, with God's help through me and, to an increasing degree, through himself, he could become self-directing. He was gaining security and independence.

One day Milt was complaining about his boss, who seemed inconsiderate and unhelpful. When Milt went to talk to him about serious matters, his boss would begin shuffling papers, reviewing notes, or looking past him, responding only with an occasional grunt.

Milt described how crushed he felt when that happened. It reminded him of the little boy he used to be, feeling worthless when his father seemed not to want to take time to talk to him or be with him. As his boss continued to ignore him, Milt would be engulfed with feelings of powerlessness and hopelessness. He would go back to his desk, discouraged and defeated, too upset to continue working until someone distracted him.

At this point, I confronted Milt. "What were you thinking about as your boss ignored you? What was your thought process? Did you allow yourself to be put down, or did you demand your boss's attention? Did your negative thoughts preclude any action?"

I had earned the right to confront Milt by carefully responding to him over the weeks. I had not betrayed his confidence, and he knew it. Thus, Milt felt secure with me and was able to investigate his feelings in the warm, open atmosphere we had developed. He began to think about and answer my questions.

Milt said he felt like a child when his boss refused to give him undivided attention. It took him back to when he was a little boy asking his father for something and finding him too busy reading the newspaper. Through a number of incidents like that, Milt had concluded, as a child, that he had no value; if he had been important, Dad would have put the paper aside and listened.

As Milt talked about that rejection, tears came to his eyes. He relived the horrible emptiness that he had felt. There had been no place to go. If he went to his mother, who always listened, his father would become angry and shout at him. If he went to his room, he would feel even more alone. So he had usually just stood there, crying inwardly. If he had cried outwardly, his father would have shouted, "You're just a crybaby! If you are going to act that way, I won't bother to come home at all."

Now the feelings of the past overwhelmed him. "Why talk about all this? It just makes me feel worse. It would be better not to bring it up at all!"

Milt's problems stemmed from reliving his past experience in the present, which prevented him from relating effectively with others. In relating to his boss, the chain reaction that bound him to the past had to be broken. In a sense, he had to become reconditioned. The emotional reliving of the past when one part of a similar present is called "redintegration."

Breaking the hold of the past is difficult. The first things the seeker needs to learn are the signs that indicate that the past is about to be replayed. For Milt, it was the first twinge of feeling rejected that started the negative spiral. From there on, negative feelings grew until they either immobilized him (as when he was with his boss) or caused him to act impulsively. The negative chain reaction blinded him to more constructive ways of reacting.

After you have earned the right, you will need, at times, to confront the one with whom you are working. With Milt, I needed to confront a negative pattern he had learned. Other people need to be confronted on their inconsistencies in behavior or outlook. You will sense, after you have worked with a person, what areas in his life contribute to his problems and need to be changed.

When confronted with what he was doing, Milt began to recognize what had been happening. He began to separate his present situation from the past and to work on changing his emotional reactions accordingly. He learned to be more assertive and found effective ways to get attention and to communicate his own point of view rather than uncritically succumbing to another's view.

Confrontation is a necessary part of effective encouragement. It may seem strange that encouragement comes from forcing a person to face a problem. Yet Scripture tells us that God disciplines those He loves (Hebrews 12:6). You and I can become instruments used by the Spirit of God to bring others' attention to deal with areas in their lives that need to be changed.

Milt's progress may seem unrealistically rapid. Actually, the changes described took place over several months of discussion and analysis. Habits that have developed over years cannot be changed overnight. That is true even of conversion. Paul points this out in his writing about the "old nature" warring with the new (Romans 7:23; Ephesians 4:24). When we are born again, the spiritual direction of our lives is completely changed. Our basic loyalties no longer belong to evil but to God. However, as Paul points out so graphically in Romans 7, the law of sin is still in us, and we must fight against it constantly.

The "law" can be called a conditioning experience. We learn to do some good things, which is great. However, some of the things we learned to do are negative and evil, and considerable attention and work are required to change them. We must learn a new set of "laws" which, when they are practiced regularly and internalized, can result in spontaneously positive behavior.

The next time Milt talked to his boss, and the boss didn't listen he said, "When I talk to you, you shuffle papers and don't listen. Then I feel like you don't care for anything I have to say. You make me feel worthless. Is that the message you want to give to me?"

Milt was changing, and because he changed, others had to change too. They couldn't stay the same. Each small facilitating effect you have on your seeker, can in the same way cause a ripple effect of changes toward more effective living. This accomplishment is really *encouraging*.

Opportunities Are
All Around Us

A few years ago, a national park ranger impressed me with the need for awareness. I was with a group he was leading on a nature walk along a gurgling mountain stream in a beautiful forest. He pointed out many obvious sights as we enjoyed our leisurely progress.

After we had walked through a meadow, he stopped and said, "Do you realize that we have tramped on some of the most beautiful creations of God? Get down on your knees and look at your footprints."

I got down and looked beneath the tall grass. There, growing in profusion, were clusters of beautiful, miniature flowers. Each cluster was different in color and shape. Some looked so delicate, it seemed that to breathe on them would destroy them. Beautiful mosses, lacy and green, were growing in the damper spots.

Some of our party sat down and talked instead of looking. They seemed not to care that they had missed this beautiful sight. The influence and encouragement of the ranger had little effect; their awareness was not increased.

But as I listened to the ranger and gazed at the beauty beneath my feet, I learned a lesson that increased my awareness of life itself. No longer could I blindly go on my way, trampling the obvious in my dealings with people. No longer could I, at least not without a prick of conscience, ignore the hidden elements of emotion and unexpressed need in their verbal messages.

As we attend to ourselves, to others, and to nature, our awareness becomes finely tuned and we begin to pick up the significant parts of seemingly aimless conversation or behavior. And as we respond to those hidden messages, we encourage and motivate the one to whom we are attending.

Becoming Aware

The first step in giving the kind of encouragement that will lead to positive changes in another's life is *attending* or listening. Attending involves both (1) paying close attention to his verbal and nonverbal messages—thus increasing your awareness of him, and (2) communicating to him that you are giving him serious attention—thus demonstrating that he is important and encouraging his own self-awareness.

When a baby cries and, in response to his cry, gets help, he learns that he can affect the people around him. He becomes aware of his capacity to influence others. If his cry is ignored, he will not learn his power to influence others. Then he may withdraw or, out of frustration, become more demanding.

Many people are unaware of their value and how they affect others. For example, the Samaritan woman with whom Jesus talked had so devalued herself that she seemed surprised that anyone, let alone a male Jew, would pay attention to her. Being noticed by someone important helped her become aware that she still had value and could influence others. Jesus' attention helped her become open to listening and responding to Him. She began to realize that He could help her. The key to the development of their relationship was Jesus' attention to her, which helped her become aware of herself.

Attending to Nonverbal Messages

Imagine Jesus' eyes holding the Samaritan woman's attention. Even though she wished to avoid discussing significant but painful details, she was compelled to continue because of Christ's attention.

There is probably no more effective way to attend and convince another of your interest than by using your senses, especially sight and hearing. A person's voice, face color, breathing, and other responses give you clues to his feelings. Respond to those clues. For example, when his voice becomes soft, respond to that change with understanding. As you notice and respond to such clues, your companion is reassured of your attention.

Each of your senses can be used to help you become more aware of the other person. Your sensory awareness and response to that awareness stimulates the other person to attend to you as well. This mutual stimulation opens doors of understanding that can make the difference between a casual encounter and a real friendship. Accurate attending can change a chance meeting into a healing and wholesome relationship.

The woman of Samaria attended to Jesus, even as he attended to her. She saw that he was a Jew, as he saw that she was a Samaritan. He wore no card around his neck saying, "I am a Jew," nor did she bear such an obvious label, but they knew that information about each other because of physical cues, and they responded accordingly.

Accurate recognition of physical cues can help you respond effectively. The person seeking help may say something seemingly insignificant but be agitated, pale, or flushed as he says it. He may breath heavily or be fidgety.

Those physical cues indicate the significance of what he is saying. As you respond to those cues, not just to the surface message, he will be reassured and feel more secure in telling you what is on his mind and in facing the issue he needs to deal with.

Communicating Attention

When the woman at the well came to draw water, Christ's attention, shown by his physical actions, made her increasingly aware of herself. He *turned* to her, *looked* at her and *spoke* to her. In doing so, he communicated to her that he was interested and was ready to listen. His encouragement demanded no specific response; she could respond in any way she wished.

Communicating to another that you are ready to attend to him is a necessary prerequisite for a relationship. You communicate that readiness by facing him, looking at him, and listening carefully to all that he has to say. You may move closer to him or lean toward him to emphasize your interest and involvement in what he is disclosing. In so doing, you encourage him to attend to what you say, as well. Your attention increases the response of the one to whom you attend, but he must *know* that you are attending to him before he will respond.

In attending, Jesus was thinking of the woman and her needs, not of whether his physical attending was making him uncomfortable. When you physically attend to another person, you focus on him, not on your own comfort. The physical tension you may feel in focusing comes across as nonverbal assurance that he has your undivided attention, which makes him more ready to communicate. Perhaps more important, the tension reminds you, also, to continue to fully attend.

Attending implies a commitment to the other person: you are ready to give acceptance, understanding, and help, if

Ready to concentrate

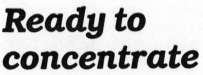

needed—in that order. That commitment is something both of you want and need, and it becomes the basis for an interchange of ideas and feelings.

Nonverbal attending communicates genuine concern and energizes mutual self-revelation. It may already be your spontaneous response to another's disclosure; but if it is not, practice until it becomes natural.

Attending Brings Response

Physical awareness of others is developed by practicing it in every situation. Sometimes awareness can be cultivated in situations that seem far removed from the counseling room.

On the woodland hike described earlier, the ranger stopped by a rock and said, "This rock can tell the secrets of the forest."

I thought, *A rock tell the secrets? Preposterous!*

But I listened and looked. The top of the rock was bare,

worn smooth by the wind and rain. Here and there in small cracks or depressions in the sides, lichens were growing unnoticed, their coloring blending in with the rock's. A little farther down the side, partially protected from the sun and wind, green mosses had begun to grow on the lichens. Farther down, grasses had added their bit to the process. As these frail plants grew, they collected the deteriorating rock from above as well as the dust from the wind to provide more soil, in which a small bush was beginning to grow.

The roots from the bush had sought out the crevices and seemed to have enlarged them. Finally, near the forest floor, a little tree had taken root and was actually splitting the rock.

The secrets of the forest? Yes. They were all there. But had we seen them at first? No. Now, with increased awareness, we could understand why the ranger was encouraging us to observe and to become aware.

In the same way, awareness of others and ourselves develops. We must expectantly look for the clues that can tell us about another. As he becomes aware of our interest and expectancy, he joins our search for meaning. The more we can see, the more we want to see, and the more we will perceive what is going on both in ourselves and in others.

When Jesus spoke to the woman at the well, her response indicated that he had passed the attention test: she began to reveal hidden aspects of her life to him. When he said, "Go call your husband," she could have replied, "You are getting too personal. I don't care to share anything more with you than the weather and places to draw water." Instead she communicated to him that she trusted Him by saying, "I have no husband." What a simple, sharp statement of her plight! So much was revealed in so little. In effect, she was saying, "I trust this man. Even though he doesn't know the sordid details of my life, he is trustworthy, and I can open myself to him."

She didn't tell everything at first, but she was ready to tell more. Jesus made the comment, she responded, and a mutual bond of trust and sharing resulted. Readiness to respond came because of encouragement.

Perhaps the person you are relating to is disturbed by the fact that life is passing by, seemingly with no purpose. He may not even be aware of his feelings of frustration about the impending end of life, but he knows he sees only dark at the end of the tunnel.

Those kinds of feelings usually are hidden from others. When you sensitively attend and respond to him, you open the door for him to reveal himself. In so doing, he and you can understand and share those hidden thoughts—bring them out in the open and talk about them—and together find some light at the end of the tunnel.

Find someone—let's call her Jane—with whom you can practice being aware and attending. Jane may be someone who is around you a lot, asking questions, trying to do things for you. Perhaps you haven't really attended to her deeper personal needs, even though you may have helped in other ways. Try to develop a healing relationship with her. The seemingly insignificant things she brings up may be tests to see what you will do. If you respond to them warmly, she will tell you more, thus indicating her growing trust in you.

Practice the skills of attending. Indicate your attention in the ways we have discussed to make her aware of your interest in her. You can't fake it; you must be truly concerned and encouraging.

Until you have practiced and learned how to be effective with someone else, you haven't mastered the skills. The feedback you get—her interest, expression of need or even rejection—will help you know whether you are really *becoming more aware* and *attending to her.*

If she responds by opening up to you, you have passed the first test. If she doesn't, you need to analyze what you are doing in order to learn better ways to relate, or to discover what is blocking you.

Attending to Yourself

When you attend to all the cues from another, you are communicating concern for him. The way you communicate concern helps him to be more explicit about himself, but even more important, you reveal something about yourself. Your behavior communicates that you are aware of him and that you really want to encourage. The desire to relate deeply with another is the prerequisite for the kind of relationship you want, but skills in communicating that desire also are necessary.

Sometimes a helper unknowingly turns people away by his physical actions or mannerisms. Therefore, examine yourself and attend to your own behavior as you attend to Jane's behavior. If you notice that people turn away from you, find out why. Perhaps you are fidgety or have mannerisms that seem to indicate impatience or inattention, and others are reacting to those mannerisms. If you become noticeably uncomfortable at the mention of certain topics, others may fear that you don't want to discuss significant concerns.

Perhaps Jane raises the question of what to do about working. You think: *This isn't important, so I'll not say much.* You say, "Well, that's a decision I can't help you with," and turn away from her.

Jane responds, "You really don't care about me, do you?"

You say, "I do—I really do!"

Jane asks, "Then why did you turn away? Why didn't you show some interest?"

Usually those you deal with aren't so frank. You may catch a hurt expression in their eyes, or they may turn away to hide their disappointment. The signs are there, verbal or nonverbal. You must become aware of them.

If Jane turns away from you, review your response. Did

you communicate to Jane through your posture and responses to sensory cues that you were interested?

Put yourself in Jane's place. Try to feel and think as she does. If you were Jane, would you see yourself as being open? Would you find yourself feeling ready to share the significant matters of your life with you? Would you, as Jane, dare to discuss very important or hurtful concerns with you? What is Jane's perception of you?

If you have effectively communicated your concern, Jane will want to reveal more of her feelings. In so doing, she will come to understand herself better. Her perception of herself will become more realistic because your feedback will help her see herself as she is, even as her responses help you see yourself from another's viewpoint.

Listen to yourself

The richness and depth of a relationship can be developed through what seem to be relatively minor responses to others, and your own life will be enriched by the mutual sharing.

When you feel uncomfortable in an exchange, listen to your inner self. If you react negatively to something, try to find out why. Take note of your feelings and actions. Try to discover *why* you do what you do when you do it. You may need to become a seeker yourself and talk to another facilitator to find out why you are uncomfortable and ineffective. Each disturbing incident gives you clues to explore. Each allows you to become more aware of yourself. Each can teach you so that you can help others more effectively. Any blind spot you have will limit your helpfulness to those who seek your aid. Self-examination is necessary for your growth as a facilitator. When you have learned how to become more aware of yourself, you will be more aware of others. It is a continuing growth process.

A Risk Worth Taking

Developing a relationship with another person as a friend or counselor can be scary! You are making yourself vulnerable. There are risks, but there also are rewards. As you become more open with others, they will become more open with you. The relationship can grow and you will become encouraging. Your responses to him communicate that he has value. That is the first level of encouraging: to make the other keenly aware of his value and to communicate that you are with him in his search for a deeper relationship. When he realizes that another will stand by and support him, his loneliness will disappear and he will be motivated to disclose himself to you and to grow.

Check Yourself

• Find someone who also is interested in learning to be an

effective encourager, and practice the skills of awareness and attending with each other. You may feel uncomfortable and mechanical at first, but if you are genuinely interested in the other person, you will soon find the skills becoming a natural part of your style as you practice.

- Does someone "bother" you often? Maybe he's a person with deep needs. Become aware of him as a person, and try to respond to his deeper, hidden needs.

- Analyze a recent experience you have had with someone. Did you really attend to him? Do you think he felt that he was the most important person in your life during your conversation? Were there any nonverbal messages that you missed?

Check your responses

- Right now attend to your own body. How does the seat of your chair feel to you? How about your hands? Do your eyes feel strained? Is your neck tense? Learn to physically attend to yourself, and you will attend more effectively to another.

How To Identify
the Needs of Others

When the Samaritan woman came to the well, she knew
only that she wanted water. But she actually had many other
needs: the need to be accepted and not rejected; the need to
be understood, not condemned; the need to be recognized as
a person with problems, not a problem person; and the need
to be recognized as valuable, not a lost soul, in spite of her
past performance. She came from a different culture but had
common needs.

Let us imagine that you, the facilitator, were to meet her
on the way to the well as Jesus did. Would you "hear" her
thoughts? If you used the attending skills described in the
last chapter, you probably would. Correctly attending to another will help him share with you the issues that are more
significant than those conveyed in such conversation as, "My,
it's hot today," or, "It's a long way to the well," or, "This road
is so dusty. I wish it would rain."

If you let simple statements like those stimulate you to
attend to what is *not* said, you will be able to respond effectively. You will begin to see as that person sees. You can hear
the hidden messages, such as: "I don't want to talk to this

person," or, "This person would condemn me if he really knew me," or, "I'm not sure that I can trust him with more than these commonplace problems." The more you concentrate on the seeker, the more ready you are to hear and understand his messages, and the more he will realize your readiness to accept even hidden thoughts and feelings.

The second step in establishing an encouraging relationship with someone seeking help is to communicate your readiness to respond. This is accomplished through listening and really hearing what he says. When you give him signs that you are truly attentive and ready to respond, he will feel free to elaborate further and to help you understand him more completely.

The first stages of a relationship set the tone for the rest. If it starts out right, the relationship becomes more satisfying and meaningful. If for some reason the relationship does not start out right, perhaps the other person is not aware that you are ready to respond to him. Making your readiness to respond clear to him is essential.

If your relationship is not going the way you want it to, stop. Examine yourself and communicate your concern with your friend. Your own readiness to explore the reasons for the difficulty will increase your awareness of each other.

Paths to Hearing

Going Further

If Jane spends time around you or has dropped in to see you, she probably has a reason. The cup of sugar she wants to borrow may be the overt reason (she may have a five-pound sack at home!), but perhaps what she really wants is someone to hear her innermost feelings. Knowing the underlying reasons she has come is important, but you won't learn about them unless you are ready to listen to far more than her immediate request for a cup of sugar.

Going further depends on establishing a relationship. Going further depends on hearing and perceiving needs behind a request. When you communicate your readiness to hear, Jane will express herself. You then can develop the relationship through effective use of your helping skills because she knows you are responding to her.

Have you really heard the needs Jane has come with? If so, you can respond so that she will share the intimate concerns of her life with you.

Isaiah voiced the hope of every encourager: "The Lord God hath given me the tongue of the learned, that I should know how to speak a word *in season* to him that is weary. . . . he wakeneth mine ear to hear" (Isaiah 50:4).

Naturally, you should not try to find hidden meanings in every casual comment, "mining" each conversation for meanings that may not be there. But it is possible to be open to unexpressed needs of great significance.

Be alert to underlying motives when a person contacts you. Assume that he had a special reason for coming to you. Respond to him as though he has more than a simple request. If you are wrong, he will correct you. If you are right, you will encourage him to express his need.

Concentrating

In order to really hear another person and help him know that you are attending, you must concentrate on what he is saying. Any distraction can cause your attention to wander, so although concentration is possible on a bus or train, choosing a place to hear that will have minimal noise or activity makes things easier.

Your place for listening should be a special place where you habitually concentrate on hearing others. It will be easier to warmly respond in this place, because you will learn to associate it with a special way of responding. It will be your "hearing place," where you concentrate on your discloser. If you want to relax or chat casually, choose another location. Reserve your hearing place for those occasions when you really want to concentrate on another's needs. Going to this place will become a signal to both yourself and the other person that you are ready to deal with matters that are important to him.

When you really concentrate on your seeker's words and feelings you are communicating, "That's it. Go on. You're on your way. I care for you."

Deliberating

Hearing requires effort not usually put forth in social conversation, where frequent interruptions are the rule. Often in a social situation, one person is thinking about what he wants to say and cannot wait for the other to stop talking before making his own comment. Because of his impatience, he does not listen to what is being said.

If during your "hearing time" you are thinking ahead to your own response, you interrupt the process of building awareness and communicating that you are willing to respond. Be careful to wait before you react to comments. Time yourself. How long can you wait, thoughtfully considering the implications of what the other person has said, before responding and yet still maintain a warm contact? (Be careful that you don't wait too long, however, or the other person may begin to wonder if you heard him. If he starts to speak again, say, "Wait a moment. I'm still thinking about what you said.")

Note the kind of response you make after deliberating. Is it different from what it would have been if you had responded immediately? You will probably find that the response you make after deliberating comes closer to meeting the need that has been expressed.

Deliberating is hard work, but it attributes value to the other person. You communicate the message that you really care about his feelings and ideas and want to encourage him in his endeavors to grow.

Responding Verbally

Responding to Facts

When we have learned how to hear with our entire being, we are ready to respond to both the feelings and the facts presented by another. Feelings are important, but facts are basic to identifying the issues, so let's look first at how to hear and respond to facts.

It is important first to be clear about the facts. Mentally summarize the facts presented and sort them out, and then respond to them individually. Ask for feedback to check your accuracy.

Here's how an encounter might progress:

Jane: "May I borrow a cup of sugar?"

Respond: "Sure. It's tough to find you are out of sugar in the middle of a project, isn't it? Is there any other way I can help?"

Jane: "Thanks—I really wanted to talk to you about a problem I have."

Wait, then respond: "I'm glad you came to me with it."

Jane: "I feel that you are willing to take the time to consider things with me."

Deliberate, then respond: "It's important for you to know that someone is ready to hear you."

Jane: "Because you are considerate and understanding, I can tell you things I wouldn't tell someone else."

Weigh, then respond: "You have confidence in me."

Notice that each response deals only with the actual content of the interchange—the facts presented—but is warm and receptive. Responding to facts reassures the seeker that his perception of reality is accurate and that someone can relate to him. When you weigh the facts, you show respect for the person presenting them.

In print, those responses may seem mechanical. But when you are deeply involved with another on a feeling level, your words will come naturally and will communicate your openness to anything the seeker has to say.

Tuning in to Feelings

As you pick up clues about how the seeker is responding, so he picks up clues from you. He knows whether you are tuned in to him. He will check to see if you are with him, if you are responding to his distress with warmth and under-standing. If you aren't or he thinks you aren't, he will soon stop being open with you.

He wants to be sure that you acknowledge his anger as valid, his happiness as realistic. You become a gauge by which he measures his perception of reality. If you tune in warmly and sensitively to his feelings, communicating by your feedback that you hear and accept his anguish and pain, you will help him gain the confidence to disclose and explore more of his feelings.

It may well be that few people have done this for Jane in the past. Many may have sympathized, but that is not really what she wants. She needs empathy, your feeling along with her and understanding her. Sympathy only reflects her prob-lems without helping her know what to do about them. When you tune in to her deeper feelings, she knows that you want to do more than just be a sounding board; you want to enter into her problems with her, to help her sort out her confused ideas and feelings and decide what to do about them.

Choosing What To Respond to

While it might be possible to respond to *all* the facts and feelings that a person talks about, to do so would take up more time than necessary and might be confusing. Usually a seeker has a particular problem he wants to talk about, and that problem area will come up repeatedly. Listen for issues that come up often and respond to them; those topics are significant. In addition, as we noted earlier, you may pick up nonverbal cues that signal that an important subject is being discussed. Respond to those cues. Zeroing in on central topics helps a person deal with them more effectively because it helps him not to be distracted by peripheral issues.

Choosing what to respond to is harder work than just commenting. It requires memory of earlier conversations to be able to recognize recurring topics. It also requires careful attention to physical aspects of the person. But don't allow the pressure of choosing to cause you to become tense in your relationship. If you zero in on the wrong thing, most people will correct you or repeat what is important. Even your mistakes can help clarify the issues for both of you.

Reread the account of Jesus' conversation with the woman at the well (John 4:7-30). What were some of the recurring themes that were significant? Write them down. Then compare your observations with mine below. But do not read on until your list is complete!

Often the circumstances or actions of the person indicate his need. For the Samaritan woman, the subject of water became the key to discerning her desire for a deeper relationship.

The woman asked for understanding. Several times she asked for clarification and more information. Her questions indicated that she wanted to know where she stood in relation to a world that condemned her—a significant need.

Her hunger for relationships came up repeatedly. Most significant, though unspoken, was her desire for a relationship with God. Her expression of surprise that she would be spoken to by a Jew, one of God's special people, indicated this need. Later, in the discussion about her husbands, her desire for a meaningful relationship appeared again. "Many" husbands had not met her need for a deep sense of belonging. The plurality of husbands in her life was a good indication of her needs.

She wanted clarification about the conflict between the Jews and Samaritans, and she expressed the hope that when the Messiah came the conflict would be settled. With that hope, she could be satisfied. Until then she wanted to know more about how she should relate and behave.

Now think about the interchanges with Jane described earlier. What were the *central* topics in all of her comments? Did the facilitator pick them out and give the best response? Perhaps you could do better.

In your daily conversations, practice choosing the significant issues and responding to them.

Checking Your Understanding

As you are building your perceptions from the information being given to you, you must check your understanding of it. Ask for feedback on the accuracy of your listening. Too often we just listen and assume that the seeker knows that we are with him. When you ask for feedback on your perception, he will be sure that you are with him, and he can correct any misperceptions you may have.

Most of us have learned to converse vaguely, making little effort to check on our understanding of the other's viewpoint. We must recondition our listening so that we can respond with accuracy. Cultivating the skill of checking allows us to do this.

One way to gain confidence that you have heard correctly and to reassure another that you have really heard his message is to feed back what he says, either by repeating his exact words or, better, by paraphrasing his meaning. Until you become proficient, it is best to stick closely to the seeker's own words.

However, merely repeating his words might give the impression that you are not carefully attending, so use introductory phrases like: "I hear you saying _____." "Is this what you said: '_____'?" "Let me repeat what you said so we can both understand clearly: '_____'." Continually using the same introductory phrases will make your responses sound stilted, so vary your

Learn to paraphrase

approach. When you feed back the speaker's words, you are demonstrating that you really want to know what he is saying.

In the following dialogue, the facilitator uses the skill of giving feedback effectively.

Jane: "I feel I can reveal myself to you more completely because I trust you."

Facilitator waits, then responds: "You can reveal yourself to me because you can trust me, is that it?"

Jane: "Yes. I'm careful about whom I talk to."

Facilitator waits, then responds: "I hear you saying that you don't talk to just anyone."

Jane: "I'll say not. Once I was really hurt by someone telling others what I had told him in confidence."

Facilitator waits, then responds: "You got hurt by trusting someone who told others?"

Jane: "That made me pretty suspicious."

Facilitator waits, then responds: "Let me repeat what you said so we'll both be sure I have it right. I understand you have become suspicious of others, and so you are careful about sharing, but you can share with me. I like that."

In your feedback, you may include observations of the person's physical state as well as your understanding of his words. In the following example, the facilitator draws on both sources of information.

Facilitator: You seem very angry about what you just said. You were even trembling a little, and your neck got red. Am I right?

Jane: Yes, you are. I didn't realize that it showed so much.

Facilitator: This issue must be pretty important to you, if you feel so strongly about it.

Jane: Yes. It makes me very upset when my husband doesn't hear what I say.

In your paraphrasing, practice translating complicated messages into simple ones without adding of your own ideas. Here is an example:

> *Jane:* I really like many things my husband does. He is kind and thoughtful and fun to be with.
>
> *Facilitator:* You like him a lot.
>
> *Jane:* Yes, but sometimes he isn't very thoughtful or helpful. Sometimes he makes me angry because he seems a long way away from us.
>
> *Facilitator:* So he's with you sometimes and sometimes he's not. And when he's not, you get angry. Is that right?
>
> [Note: both ideas are paraphrased]
>
> *Jane:* It's the uncertainty of it all that gets to me. I expect him to be the way I want him to be, and then he's not there. Fortunately, he's really there sometimes when I don't expect it.
>
> *Facilitator:* Do I hear you saying that you can't be sure of how your husband will react?
>
> *Jane:* Yes, I guess that's it.

When you check your perception by paraphrasing, your partner feels understood. He will be encouraged by your observations and want to go further in building your relationship.

To summarize, *paraphrasing* involves:

1. Saying what you think you heard, usually in fewer words.
2. Asking for feedback on the accuracy of your perception of what was said.
3. Giving the person a chance to correct your perception (at first you may have to ask for that correction; later, he will correct spontaneously).

Does paraphrasing seem unnatural? As you see its effect on others, you will become more spontaneous and natural with it.

Remember, the seeker would not be coming to you if he were not motivated to do something about his problems. You help him by constantly checking on the accuracy of your perceptions, because as you do so, he also checks on his own communication. A clear interchange encourages further exploration of thoughts and feelings.

Nonverbal Elements of Responding

Matching Speed and Loudness

Earlier you were advised to hesitate before responding to a seeker's statement. As you get to know him better, you can begin to respond more quickly. However, you should *match* your response to the seeker's expressions. For example, if he speaks slowly and hesitantly, you likewise should speak slower. If you were to respond rapidly, with a smooth flow of words, the contrast between his and your styles of speech might be disturbing instead of helpful. When you match your tempo of speech with your friend's, he will recognize that you are accepting and responding to him as he is. If you respond differently, he may not go on and develop his thoughts more completely, and you will be unable to relate deeply and effectively.

Another characteristic you might need to match is the loudness of his voice. If your friend talks in a whisper and you respond loudly, the contrast will be disturbing. (However, if he speaks very loudly and you respond normally, he may tone down his voice and perhaps become more attentive, so a contrast can sometimes be useful.)

Matching or contrasting the speech speed and loudness of your speech to that of your friend will convey the message that you are really trying to relate to him.

Matching Emotional Intensity

As a person talks, his emotional intensity will give you an

indication of the seriousness of the problem to him. Rapid breathing, blushing, and a tremulous voice are all external indicators of his depth of feeling. Your response should reflect your awareness of that depth.

If your friend is very serious, you should be serious. When he is joyful, you should respond with joy. Although you cannot and need not reproduce such physical symptoms as

blushing and rapid breathing, your approximation of his intensity in your voice and in other physical responses will communicate to him that you are involved in his needs. Matching his intensity confirms that you accept the importance of what he is saying and see him as a person of value. When he knows through his experience with you that you are genuinely interested in him as a person and not as a "case," he will gain the security to explore his problems further. He will be encouraged by your indications that you *care*.

Matching Vocabulary

A seeker may use vocabulary different from your own. Although identically matching the words of another is impossible, you need to adjust your usual vocabulary to approximate his. For example, if he uses simple words and you choose long, complicated ones, you may become obfuscatory and disconcerting. (See what I mean?) While you need not go to the extent of using poor grammar or profanity, the closer you approximate his vocabulary style, the more helpful you can be. You confirm his worth at his present state of growth when you accept his style of expression.

On the other hand, you might want to deliberately contrast your style of speech with his. A facilitator can move somewhat beyond the seeker's patterns and be a stimulating model. You may wish to speak a little faster, using slightly more complicated words, to give him a goal for improvement. If he speaks very rapidly and uses complicated terminology, you might speak more slowly and simply to help him achieve clarity.

It may seem to you that attempts to match another person's speed, loudness, intensity, and vocabulary are insignificant in developing a relationship. But remember, the goal you are striving for is to make the other person feel comfortable and secure in your interchange. Anything you can do

Reinforcing non-verbally

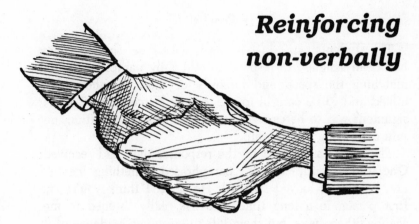

toward that goal will be helpful and encouraging to him.

Reinforcing Security

Most behavior continues because it is reinforced. If an individual were not reinforced for his actions, he would stop them. We're not always aware of the payoff for our actions, though. The relationship you establish with your friend can become the context in which he discovers what is reinforcing his problem behaviors.

When you communicate your desire to help, respond to your friend where he is, and give feedback to help him understand himself better, you are reinforcing his efforts to change. At the same time, you are motivating him and giving him a sense of security that allows him to explore and deal with aspects of himself that until now have been too painful to acknowledge.

A growing relationship involves increasingly intimate sharing. As the seeker shares, and discovers, to his relief, that what he says is accepted by you, he gains the security to move ahead to matters that he has avoided sharing with any other person. Your offering of security promotes growth, and you are an *encourager*.

It Works!

The students came in bouyantly, with faces shining. They had been assigned to respond to others by paraphrasing and matching the speed and intensity of those to whom they talked and to be careful to check their perceptions. This assignment was to be carried out in ordinary conversation, not in a counseling relationship.

They were astounded by the responses they had received. One student said, "When I paraphrased something Joe told me, he almost looked shocked. He said, 'I think you're the first person in a long time who has really listened to me. Maybe others have, but they didn't give much evidence of it, like you did.' When Joe said that, I really began to understand what we have been talking about in this class. Joe seemed to come alive, and we talked about things he said he had seldom shared with anyone else."

Another student said, "When I tried to listen for the way a person talked and then matched his speed and intensity, he seemed to listen to me more. Before, my ideas seemed to go over his head, but when I tried to match him, he somehow got the feeling that I really cared for him and his ideas. That was great!"

Another reported, "I had to *stop* paraphrasing and *matching* verbal expressions—I got into such long and deep conversations that I had no time to study! When I was open and honest in my sharing, my friend responded the same way. We discovered things about each other that we had never known before. It was exciting, but it was also time consuming. You really have to care for someone to go into things that deeply!"

Check Yourself

- Think about a relationship you are now developing. Have you been alert to underlying messages in the other person's words and behavior? Have you communicated your readiness to hear and respond to those messages?

- Choose a "hearing place" and begin to make it a point to use it when dealing with someone who is seeking encouragement. Note the difference that the absence of distraction makes in your relationship.

- Review the various skills involved in hearing and responding to another's need: going further, concentrating, deliberating, repeating and paraphrasing both facts and feelings, choosing what to respond to, and matching nonverbal qualities. Then practice those skills with someone who is willing to explore himself, taking turns being the seeker and the facilitator. Tape record your interchange, and play it back to see how effective you were in your listening and responding.

4

Take Off Your Mask

The deep kind of listening and understanding we've been looking at is not the usual way in which people relate to each other. In fact, it can be rather threatening to both parties. Most of us have been schooled *not* to listen with understanding, so we usually have distorted pictures of each other. We are unsure of our own and others' reality.

Being open means that your motivations and desires are clear to another person. The facade you usually wear is stripped away. In open, honest communication, both you and the seeker stand before each other without pretense, without masking your true feelings.

It is comforting to the seeker to know that you care enough to go to the trouble of being open and honest with him. Knowing that, he is sure that you accept him as he is, and he wants to be open as well.

Genuineness

Taking Off the Mask

"He who persists in genuineness will increase in adequacy." Being genuine is being yourself. A genuine person avoids posturing and masking his real personality. He has no need to hide some part of himself. He is who he is.

I once saw a painting of two people. They were naked but not really exposed to each other, because each held a mask in front of his face. They communicated mask to mask, not person to person.

What kind of effective communication can take place mask to mask? Responses would always miss the point. When my son was in Europe, we grew in our understanding of each other through our letters, but we were always a few weeks behind in our responses to each other's new insights. That is what communicating mask to mask is like.

A relationship must be based on who we are, naturally and honestly. Genuine relating requires being nondefensive when attacked or confronted and being ready always to examine and reexamine our assumptions and ideas.

As you increase in genuinely being yourself, you will find yourself learning and growing, and you won't want to "act as if." Can you be as open with your friend as you want him to be with you? When you encourage in that loving, affirming way, you become a model for the seeker; when you face a person honestly, he learns to face himself with honesty. Because he feels good about the way you treat him, he tries to become genuine with you as well as with himself and others.

When you listen to some testimonies or observe people in churches today, you might receive the impression that few Christians ever have a problem. We want to convince everyone that everything is all right with us—because if it isn't, we aren't living the Victorious Christian Life.

When those who do have problems—and know it—see only the happiness, joy, and growth in another's life, they begin to think there must be something wrong with themselves. They must not be doing things right.

Several years ago I wrote an article about Christian facades, "Dishonesty on Cloud Nine." A copy of it ended up in Indonesia, where a missionary read it. He thought, *Am I doing that? Am I conveying the impression of a problem-free life?*

He decided to try letting his mask down. Here is what he wrote about the results:

> As you know, Mary and I are from ancestry, where folk do not wear their hearts on their sleeves. In fact, they are ultra-reserved when it comes to expressing emotion of any kind. Well, Mary and I may have inherited some of that characteristic. And I recently realized that this can be a form of "cloud nine dishonesty."
>
> While counseling a discouraged staff member one day, I shared some personal discouragement that I was experiencing. He lit up like a neon sign and exclaimed, "You mean *you* have times of discouragement, too?" He went on to say that his own discouragement had been multiplied by the way Mary and I *seemed* always to be "on top." We never *seemed* to have any problems or to be down in the dumps about anything.
>
> I apologized for our deception, because nothing could have been further from reality. Honestly revealing myself to that staff member seemed to be the very medicine he needed to help him on his way to self-acceptance.

When it is appropriate and we remove our "I'm all OK" masks, we open the way for others to show us how they really feel, too. When you are sure that the time is right for you to share your feelings, be open and honest. It is one of the best ways of being an encourager.

When you are genuine, you are not playing the role of facilitator; you are being yourself—a helping, healing person. When you are puzzled, you share your puzzlement and don't pretend you understand or have an answer. When you feel sure of an insight, you say so, but qualify your statement by acknowledging that it's your own hunch and may

Can
I risk
exposing
myself?

not really apply to the seeker.

It will be hard for both you and your friend to drop your masks. Yet they must be removed as much as possible in order for both of you to deal effectively with his needs. When in response to your genuineness he allows himself to be seen as he really is, he will be so relieved at not having to pretend that he will be motivated to be even more open and honest. You, as facilitator, can join him in sharing that wonderful experience of a genuine relationship.

Sharing Through Self-Disclosure

As you relate to another, your own feelings will inevitably be stirred. When it is appropriate, share them. If you have had similar experiences, share how you felt and perhaps how you dealt with them. A valid indicator of your own receptiveness to another is your openness in sharing with him.

A word of caution, however. If you end up talking more than the other person, the distinction between you, the facilitator, and the seeker may become blurred. Always remember, *he* is the one who is there to be helped; any sharing you do must be for the purpose of helping him, not yourself. Your openness must be designed to help him become more open so that you can respond to his needs.

Jesus was open with the Samaritan woman about his need for water. His openness created a common ground for discussion, because they had a common need. If he had not confessed his need, there might never have been a conversation or a decision. Because he was honest and straightforward with her, she could eventually share her deeper needs, and he could help her discover the answer to those needs.

Your sharing may be brief, often only hinting at a need or feeling you have. But it will encourage the seeker to be honest in sharing with you. Genuine self-disclosure can be one of the most effective means to be an encourager.

Because Jesus was open about his needs, the water that he asked for became the focus of a lively discussion. She was surprised that he would talk to her. That beginning led into a discussion of spiritual water, which confused her but opened the door to further exploration. Both his needs and hers were revealed through a simple discussion of water.

It's time for self-examination. The Psalmist said, "Search me and know my heart; test my thoughts" (Psalm 139:21). Now you, with God's help, can search yourself. Are you nervous when you begin to be more genuine with another person? Are there blocks that seem to get in the way of stripping off your mask? Are you afraid of becoming honest with yourself and others?

Studies have shown that people who are afraid of exposing themselves—sharing how they feel, right here and now—

discourage others from being open and honest. Naturally, it wouldn't be appropriate to "spill your guts" to everyone you meet. But can you, when it is appropriate, share yourself at a deeper level with others? Can you tell them how you feel, what the relationship means to you, how you deal with problems similar to theirs?

People who are self-disclosers invite self-disclosure of others. Have you noted how some people attract others in a more personal way? That is evidence of being a *discloser.*

As you become used to responding to others with openness and honesty, your fears of self-disclosure will begin to dissolve. You will feel more secure and, as a result, the seeker also will feel more secure and more ready to explore himself. That's real encouragement!

Being Willing to Be Human

Once, on a bus from the San Francisco to the Oakland Airport, I asked a Chinese man, "Alan," about the bus route. Alan answered my question, and then pointed to a sign behind him, which also answered my question! I commented on my skills of observation, and we both laughed. Then we began talking about many things—jobs, places we had been, our families.

Because I responded encouragingly to his ideas, Alan began to feel more comfortable with me. As he relaxed, I did too. Our sharing went deeper. Soon he asked if I had any children. When I said I had three living sons, he wanted to know how old they were and what they did. As I revealed more of myself, he was encouraged to reveal more of himself—as often happens in open communication.

Eventually Alan shared some feelings about his wife, who worked for the same company as he. He was proud of that company and was happy that they both worked there. But then he spoke of his desire to have a family, and his voice was tinged with hurt. He wanted a child, but they were un-

able to have one. He wondered if it was his wife's fault or
his. He was concerned about the effect of this problem on
their relationship.

All of this came out in the space of thirty minutes, during
which time we had traveled only a few miles. How did this
depth of sharing happen so quickly? Chinese people are often hesitant to talk about themselves. Why wasn't Alan?

Let's analyze the interchange. It opened with an expressed
need—a genuine one—"How can I get from here to there?"
Often we are hesitant to ask for help from another. It feels
safer to go to an official, who may curtly answer the question and dismiss us. Asking from another encourages relationships.

It started humorously. We joked about my overlooking the
sign that gave the information I needed.

We were both open to our environment. Things that were
going on around us prompted conversation.

And I demonstrated openness to Alan. As I shared things
about myself, he responded by sharing things about himself.
A feeling of trust developed because of each other's encouragement. Eventually Alan was sharing some of his deepest
concerns—with one who had been a complete stranger half
an hour earlier!

Nonjudgmental Acceptance of Others

When Christ met and talked with the woman at the well,
he at first did not confront her with her past. You, the facilitator, should do the same. You assure your friend, through
words and action, that he is valuable and worthwhile regard-
less of past immature or immoral behavior. Initially, you
should set down requirements for his response or improvement. After he becomes secure in the relationship, he will be
ready to think about making changes and listen to your direction. You may eventually need to confront him about his
past to demonstrate real caring; but at first, encourage.

Our realization of God's love is an apt parallel. When we experience God's love, we can in turn love others. That love will be expressed in nurturing others—giving them physical, emotional, and spiritual nourishment. Jesus said that even a cup of cold water, given in the spirit of involvement and concern, "in my name," is meaningful. Giving a cup of water (or coffee) to a person may be the nourishing gesture he

Open to share

needs. Finding a quiet place where you can attentively listen can also begin to meet the need for nurturance. Your openness and freedom from distraction allow your friend to express his needs to you.

Feedback Conveys Acceptance

When you verbally feed back facts and feelings in a way

that conveys warmth and understanding, you demonstrate noncondemning acceptance of the seeker. Early in the relationship, you must hold back your evaluation of the other person's behavior and words. When he sees that what he tells you is not being judged, he will feel free to be open and honest with you. When you allow his message to sink in, you will find yourself becoming more understanding and nonjudgmental, and when you are nonjudgmental, you become more open and honest as well. Your openness will help further increase your friend's openness.

You need not feel a "responsibility" to question or condemn what he is saying. If you have established an atmosphere of acceptance, he will probably begin to question and evaluate his actions and words himself. He had misgivings about his thinking and behavior before he came to see you; otherwise, he would not be there. And if he has done wrong, others have probably already condemned him, so he doesn't need your condemnation. In fact, condemnation may well have been his only experience until his encounter with you. So be noncondemning in both word and behavior.

Do you find yourself inwardly evaluating and judging others? If you are doing it silently, you are communicating that judgment without realizing it. "Judge not lest ye be judged," Scripture reminds us.

Forgiveness Opens the Way for Growth

A significant demonstration of the noncondemning attitude Jesus had toward the Samaritan woman was his ability to forgive her past mistakes. Because he was God, he had the authority to forgive her directly.

None of us can forgive another for what he has done to others, but you *can* help another to know that you cherish him as a person of value. You can help him temporarily look beyond his past mistakes and maladjustments. You can help him take the attitude, "I goofed back there. I can't do any-

thing about it here and now, but I will get back to that problem soon. Right now I have to learn how to deal with present problems in ways that are helpful. When I have learned,
then I can go to the next step and make past mistakes right."

By overlooking the past and being encouraging, you help
another to concentrate on his present problems. At the same
time, you discourage "hamper dumping," the hurried review
of all past problems, which often results only in overwhelming discouragement. You communicate to the seeker that you
are concerned about responding to him in the here and now
and will help him review the past when he is ready. Temporarily overlooking the past will help him forgive himself
when it is appropriate and perhaps will help him realize and
accept God's forgiveness without reservation. In a deep, caring relationship, you can communicate God's love for a hurting person in a tangible way.

Alan and I were sharing many thoughts and ideas on our
bus ride to the Oakland Airport. Suddenly we realized we
weren't sure where we were to transfer to the train. A beard-
ed man in jeans, "Jim," heard our expressions of confusion.
Jim knew the way and told us how to proceed.

Just then we were passing through a city full of cemetar-
ies. A woman behind us said, "Now I'll know what my kids
mean if they tell me to go to this city. They'll really mean
they want to get rid of me!"

We all laughed. Jim moved across the aisle to sit next to
us. He said he had read in the local paper about a man who
had decided that when he died, he wanted to be cremated,
have his ashes mixed in San Francisco sourdough bread, and
have the bread fed to the pigeons on Union Square. We all
laughed about that together and began to talk about other
things.

As Jim entered into our rapport, he began revealing some
of his struggles. He was a Greek Orthodox priest and minis-
tered to the street people of San Francisco. He was strug-

gling to discover what he should do, where he should go, where he should live.

We reached our transfer point, and Margaret, who had been quietly listening, gave us directions and helped us transfer. Alan got on one train and Jim on another. Margaret and I boarded a train and discovered it was the same one Jim had boarded.

It didn't take long to get back to our conversation. Street ministries are among the hardest to be involved in. Jim shared his feelings about the tension, pressure, and danger that seemed to threaten his very being. He was tempted to retreat into a monastery and spend his life in safe contemplation—but that didn't seem right.

We communicated our concern for him and helped him to go further. As he did, he began to weigh his alternatives. Could he be satisfied away from the active, involved life that he had been living? On the other hand, how long might it be before one of the street people put a knife into him and ended it all? We helped him sort out the important aspects of his decision making.

As we reflected his thinking back to him, without his even being aware of it, he began to understand himself better. Some of his hidden fears emerged, were examined, and were dealt with by exposure to our consideration and scrutiny. He was weighing the facts and discovering what was involved in each choice.

Soon it was time for another transfer. Margaret and I changed trains and Jim went on to his way, still thinking about the alternatives available to him. None of us was fully aware that the techniques of encouragement had been used in our conversation and that they had changed a casual encounter into a meaningful relationship.

Now Margaret and I were alone on the train bound for the airport. At my request, she explained where I should go when I got off the train. Then we reviewed the interesting conversations that had taken place. She didn't know much about Alan, so we concentrated on Jim—reviewing his problem, wishing we had had more time to discuss his concerns.

Then, rather suddenly, she said she had a real problem with her daughter. Her daughter was headstrong and wouldn't listen to Margaret. She had urges that were beyond her years. She had quit school at age 16, saying that it was boring and she wasn't learning anything. She had been planning to become an attorney, but dropping out of school seemed to cut off that possibility.

Gradually, as Margaret talked, I helped her to weigh the facts about her child. She and her husband were worried about the situation. I was noncondemning, although I suspected they were handling the situation poorly. Had I been confrontive at that point, however, our conversation would have stopped; but because I overlooked the points of disagreement and difference for the moment, I was able to be for Margaret an encourager.

As she talked about the things her daughter was doing, I repeated by paraphrasing her ideas. When she realized that I had really heard what she was saying, she corrected and clarified the responses so that I could understand. She felt totally accepted and therefore wanted me to know more; in turn, I could be of more help in her understanding.

I carefully chose what I responded to, and we moved rapidly on in our discussion.

I had formed some hypotheses about both Margaret and her husband. I even had several about their daughter. I began to share some of my ideas with Margaret. Her daughter must be intelligent; they might encourage her to develop her intelligence apart from school for the moment, not losing sight of her ultimate goal. Working at some menial job might bring perspective back to her, making school not seem so bad! Based on the clues that Margaret had given, I also suggested ways that she might change her responses to her daughter to defuse her defensiveness and anger toward the demands being made on her.

As our train ride ended, Margaret said, "If I can encourage my daughter as you have me in this short bus and train ride, maybe she'll come to her senses!"

We had moved from discussing my need for direction to Margaret's deep but hidden worries about her daughter in about one hour of seemingly casual conversation.

How did it happen? Each of the principles was used— encouragement to go further, concentration on what was being said, deliberation, hearing, openness, and nonjudgmental acceptance of personal struggle. That changed chance meetings into a meaningful interchange that affected each one of us.

This kind of interchange can be the experience of an *encourager*. As you practice and develop your own skills in encouragement, you will find doors of conversation and response opening to you as well. You may ultimately find yourself confronting others and sharing your own personal faith and life experience. You will be an *encourager*.

Cultural Sensitivity

Meeting people from different cultures requires a special kind of awareness and sensitivity of the kind just described. When you don't understand all of the nuances of meaning, or the ways that people of a different culture respond, these techniques of paraphrasing and giving feedback take on additional force and meaning. When you are open, the national can tell you how to respond, and clarify misconceptions. Knowing that you will be corrected gives you the freedom to be more expressive and increase your understanding.

Check Yourself

• Ask a close friend to give you honest feedback on how

much and how genuinely you share yourself in a relationship. Do you need to increase or improve your self-disclosure?

• Think of a time recently when you were fairly criticized. What was your response? Were you defensive? Did you try to cover up your mistake? Or were you able honestly to accept the negative feedback and grow from it?

• When someone begins to disclose something—especially something painful—to you, note whether he continues to talk about it, or stops talking or changes the subject. If he stops his disclosure, check with him to find out if you were giving any nonverbal messages that discouraged him from continuing. If you were, examine yourself to find out how you really feel about what he was disclosing. Don't encourage him to continue unless you can genuinely accept what he is saying.

• The next time you have a casual conversation with someone, see if you can help dissolve the barriers to true revelation by the means that have been discussed and that worked so well with Allan, Jim and Margaret. Then you may be able to help them consider what Christ can do in their own lives, and become more effective witnesses for God.

5

What's Happening Behind the Scenes?

Few privileges in life are more exciting than entering into the life experience of another person. Becoming sensitively aware of another allows you to help him deal more effectively with his problems and life, no matter what cultural background he has.

Likewise, nothing is more fulfilling than sharing your own life fully in building a relationship. When someone else truly knows you—all the good and bad—and chooses to be with you in a caring relationship, life truly can become full and rich. When you have this kind of acceptance, you can offer it to another. Even though you as a facilitator do not reveal yourself totally, your sensitive self-disclosure implies that you have committed yourself to being actively involved in an encouraging relationship.

Up to this point, we have seen that by carefully listening and attending to another person, you come alive—become fully aware of and responsive to—his needs. You hear and understand what he is saying. You develop skills of perception that help you understand him. At the same time, your friend also is becoming more aware of himself as a person. He is reassured of his value, and because you are receptive, he opens up to you. Through your interaction he begins to identify and recognize his needs, and he becomes willing to acknowledge areas in his life that need changing.

The purpose of reassurance and support is to give the person the security to explore himself further so that he can understand himself better and begin to take tentative steps toward changing his behavior. The way you relate to him serves as a model for him. When you respond to him as able, worthwhile, and valuable, he believes you and begins to believe he can change. Modifying your behavior so that the "fruit of the Spirit" (love, patience, kindness and gentleness) can be seen in your own life, encourages their development in the seeker's life. You make the love of God more tangible to him, and you open the way for him to trust both you and God. Your next step is to respond to the seeker in ways that induce better self-understanding so that any changes he makes will be realistic and in keeping with his abilities.

Perceiving

Perceiving means that you as facilitator attend, listen, and hear. But even more, it means that you help the seeker put things together. That's being an *Encourager*. There are many disparate elements in conversation. One of your challenges is to help bring those disparate elements together, making a comprehensible whole. You need to check constantly to determine if your own perception of the whole picture is correct.

Communication usually goes beyond words themselves. Each thought and word is a revelation, a window into the inner world of the speaker, somewhat different in each culture, but with common human experience underneath it all. Our human needs for love, recognition and encouragement are beyond cultures, though the ways of meeting them may be different somewhat.

The *denotative* meaning of a word is the bare skeleton of a dictionary definition. *Connotative* meaning adds the richness of personal and cultural experience. When we respond only to the denotative meaning, we miss much and come across as cold. Listen for the connotative meanings in what is said. Your friend really wants to know if you can hear and understand him better than others do. Capturing that inner meaning makes an interchange exciting. Through good communication you focus in on how a person feels about himself and his world, and you better understand his way of life.

When you give evidence that you are perceiving what he is, he feels that you really begin to know who he is.

That feeling of being known is comforting. It gives him a positive grounding in reality. More, it motivates him to be even more transparent so that you can know him even better. He wants to communicate across whatever barriers there are between you.

Increased perception results in more accurate feedback. As you both are open and honest, your relationship will become richer and fuller, because you will know more about each other.

Advanced Empathy: Expanding on Feelings

Responding to the feelings of others helps them understand themselves, but your feelings during the interchange also are important.

As a person tells about his experiences, listen carefully to yourself as well as to him. Ask yourself how his words make you feel. Your own feelings as you react to him help you understand his feelings. Your empathy with another increases as you respond with accuracy. Feed back the gist of the feelings being stirred up within you so the other person can correct or confirm the impressions you are getting from him.

Jane: I'm at a loss as to what I should do. Everything seems to be slipping away from me, and I'm really getting anxious.

Can you empathize with her? Empathy involves vicarious experiencing—putting yourself in the place of another and feeling with her. Or it can be "feeling into," as does a spectator who moves rhythmically to music being played. How do you feel about what Jane said? Can you experience that feeling both intellectually and emotionally? If so, how would you respond?

Facilitator: You're really confused, and it seems that everything is slipping from your control, which is upsetting. Is that it?

Does that relect the feelings you experienced in response to Jane? How would you phrase it? Try it out, and check with others to see how they would respond.

Drawing on your own feelings as you respond to another moves him along in self-exploration. His responses will help you clarify your own understanding and enable you to become more active in encouraging him to do something about his problems.

"Feeling into" What Another Says

Reacting to a person's feelings and to your own helps you to identify with the person with whom you are building a relationship. Some years ago, a man said that no one can really understand the Indian unless he has walked in his moccasins. The implication is that you have to experience what another has experienced in order to really know what the other person feels and knows.

There is validity in that statement, although it is impossible to experience the entire lives of everyone seeking help. However, using *sharing words*—words that aim at participating in another's feelings—can allow you to "feel into" the life of another. One psychotherapist called this an attempt at trying to live inside the skin of another.

Whatever the problem, if a person believes that you are trying to help and to experience life as much as possible *in the way he does*, he will be stimulated to experience his own life more fully and to help you experience it with him.

The detail with which a person explores himself will show how well you are "feeling into" his life. Your feeling with him rewards him for his efforts at self-disclosure and motivates him to keep on revealing himself, even though the subject matter may be painful and difficult to discuss.

Communicating Advanced Empathy

You already have learned that when a person reveals himself to you, it is helpful to reflect his feelings by a paraphrase or a simple restatement of what he has said. That is matching your response to the feelings being expressed.

In advanced empathy, you begin to expand on those feelings by describing them. For example, Jane comes to you and says she feels confused. Now ask yourself: How does confusion make me feel? Confusion may make you feel frustrated, as it does most people. What does that frustration lead to? Often to anger or discouragement over the difficulty of finding solutions. Therefore, an advanced empathic response might be, "You feel frustrated, angry, discouraged." If you hit the mark, you are responding to your friend's deeper feelings, a rewarding experience for both of you. If you are wrong, she can correct you and perhaps clarify for herself what her deeper feelings are. In either case, the attempt is rewarding.

Another example: Jane comes to you expressing pleasure because something she did turned out well. Ask yourself: How does that make me feel? In similar situations, you would probably feel joyful and excited. So you can say, "You feel happy—on top of the world!"

We all have our ups and downs. When someone comes to share his experiences with you and you respond to his feelings, you help him to come alive to himself and understand himself better. He may respond, "You help me to talk about my feelings, put handles on them. I can understand them better!"

Reinforce the positive steps that Jane makes. Behavior that is reinforced will continue. Responding to feelings by describing them is one way to reinforce the seeker's and your own understanding. You will find joy not only in Jane's success but also in your own achievements as a facilitator.

Moving Ahead

Each skill that we practice allows us to become more effective in our relationships. Sometimes we have to become more active. For example, we may have to move ahead of a person, inviting further expression. It is like throwing a ball to the place you think the running child will be by the time the ball gets there: You anticipate where he is going and jump ahead to that place, in anticipation of his thoughts. If you are wrong, he will correct you. Some call this "forming hypotheses" about the person, or "leading." When you have developed an hypothesis, you test it by asking for confirmation. Here are some examples:

> It seems to me, from what you have said, that your relationship with your father affects your relationship with all those in authority. Does that make sense to you?

> Am I right in thinking that you are allowing your relationship with that particular boy to affect your feelings about all boys?

Leading a person is always risky, for he may think you are forcing him to go in a direction that he doesn't want to go and may be resentful. However, if you give him responsibility for accepting or rejecting your ideas, leading can result in increased understanding for both of you.

Following are some cautions for leading:

1. Always check your reason for going ahead. Be certain that you are not just being unsure or impatient.
2. Be tentative, not dogmatic, in your phrasing.
3. Wait for the seeker to pick up or reject what you have presented to him.
4. In a cross-cultural setting, be especially careful with leading. Always request feedback and clarification.

Jesus used leading in talking with the woman at the well. When she asked him for the water that would eternally satisfy thirst, he said, "Go call your husband." He was moving ahead of her. He confronted her with her immorality before he answered her question. In doing so, he helped her see that the concept of spiritual water was not to be taken lightly, and he encouraged her to move on in her understanding.

Indirect Leading

When you go beyond what a person has said, you encourage him to explore further. It is important, however, that the person himself feel responsible for the direction of the interview. Your leading, therefore, should be indirect much of the time.

At the beginning of an interview, open-ended questions such as, "What's on your mind?" "Where are you in your thinking today?" "What brought you here?" will encourage the seeker to take responsibility for what is to be discussed. Later in the interview you might say, "Tell me more about—," "You mentioned earlier—" "I'd like to hear more about—," thus giving a little more direction to the interview.

Sometimes a seeker may become angry because he expects you, the "expert," to take more of a lead and even to give him advice. You might respond by explaining that no one knows about himself better than he does, so it is up to him to take the initiative. You, as facilitator, are there to help him gain new insights, but in the final analysis, he must be the judge of the course of action. He has to live with his decisions—you don't!

Leading indirectly encourages the person to assume personal responsibility for exploring himself.

Clarifying

When you go beyond what a person says—making a guess or hypothesis about his message—you are offering an idea to him that may clarify his more complicated feelings. If he rambles, giving you too many ideas to sort out, you can ask him to clarify what is most important. You might say, "I can't quite keep up with all the ideas you are presenting to me. Could you give me an illustration that will help me understand?"

Such a request forces him to clarify—both to you and to himself—what he is trying to say. It slows his presentation enough that he can think over what he is saying.

In other cases you might ask him to rephrase what he is saying. "You seemed to be trying to focus on something, but your ideas are coming too fast. Can you rephrase the concept you are trying to get across to me?"

In some cases, you might paraphrase what you heard and then ask for clarification. "I get the idea that you feel unsure of yourself in many situations, but I don't quite understand the reason you gave for it. Could you tell me about it in another way?"

When your request for further information helps a person understand himself and his world, you become more than just a reflector, you are an Encourager.

Inquiring

Your own lack of understanding of what a person is saying can become the basis for inquiring further about an idea presented. Open-ended questions (questions that cannot be answered yes or no) will lead to more complete explanations. When you ask questions that allow a one-word answer, the only way you can get more information is to ask more questions. You will soon feel as if you are playing a game of Twenty Questions, with the responsibility on you, the facilitator, to figure out the problem and fill in the silences.

When your questions require more than one word for a response, you put the responsibility of exploration on the seeker. He will need to look at himself more carefully to find out why he reacts or feels as he does.

Usually questions beginning with *what* or *how* cannot be answered by a simple yes or no. Questions beginning with *is* and *are* often can. Here are some examples of open-ended questions:

"What is meant by your anger just now?"

"How can you relate this problem to others?"

"In what ways do you respond differently now than before?"

"In what ways do you handle these problems in your country?"

If Jane expresses anxiety about her child's growing independence, you might ask, "How does your husband fit into this?" "Explain more about your relationship with your husband." "Where do you find your value as a person?"

Such questions require Jane to take responsibility for discovering why she feels the way she does about her child's independence and help her to know herself better. Thus the questions are for Jane's benefit, not just to satisfy your own curiosity. In questioning, follow these principles:

1. Inquire about the *feelings* expressed, not just content.
2. Use questions that help the seeker understand himself rather than only helping you understand him.
3. Use questions that are relevant to the subject at hand.

Remember, the goal of your interchange is to increase each other's understanding. Even our questions can be an indication of our caring for the other person, since the more we care, the more we want to know. Inquiring thus can be valuable to the growth of your relationship with a special friend or with someone who comes to you for help.

Singling out one point in the conversation and asking about it often helps a person be more explicit about the possible causes of his feelings. Zeroing in like that can help clear up confusion and vagueness both for you and for him.

It is important to remember that confusion about the information may be only your own. You must be discriminating with your questions, and ready to learn.

Focusing

As the relationship grows, you the facilitator may note a special need to focus on a statement that you think is worth further exploration. When your friend is rambling, focusing may give needed direction to what he is saying. Aimless conversation can confuse both of you. Focusing on one thought helps the communciation and reinforces the importance of an idea.

Sometimes you may need to ask your friend to identify what he considers most important in what he has been talking about. For example, you may say:

"You have been saying a lot just now. What do you think is most important to you?"
"I'd like to know more about your feelings about your older brother."
"Tell me more about your relationship with your Dad. That seems significant."

Focusing helps the seeker face and deal with an issue he may be hesitant to discuss. Some guidelines for focusing are:
1. Focus when you feel you do not understand. If you are confused, the seeker may be also.
2. Watch for clues to what is important to the seeker.

3. Help the person focus on the feelings reflected in his conversation.

Be alert to the priority your seeker places on the subject. Zero in on those ideas that you think *he feels* are important, even though he may not say so. As we have seen already, repetition of a theme is one indication of its importance. Emotional overreaction to an experience described is another. As you respond to those clues and probe further, you will recognize their significance. Your initial confusion has thus given you direction for proceeding to focus on a subject.

Check Yourself

- Make an outline of the skills of advanced empathy presented in this chapter, and practice them with a friend. Get feedback from each other on the accuracy and depth of your understanding.

- Review a recent conversation. Can you pick out the essence of what the other was saying?

- The next time you find yourself not understanding what another is saying, or you feel he himself is not aware of the real point of what he is saying, practice using open-ended questions to clarify the issues. Note whether your questions lead him as well as yourself to better understanding.

- Practice the skills of paraphrasing and clarifying in your conversation with many people. What effect does it have on your relationships?

The Turning Point and How To Perceive It

When you have communicated to your friend that you will listen and be nonjudgmental, you have earned the right to be confrontive with him. When he is convinced of your genuineness and honesty, he is ready to confront you as well, which should be encouraged.

Mutual confrontation leads to the deepest and most rewarding kind of relationship. You can speak more freely and directly, knowing that if you are off base, he will tell you. He also can speak freely, knowing that you will respond with your insights or disagreement. That is real freedom in a relationship. It is at this point that you may be able to voice your differences in outlook and your convictions about life.

Being effective in confrontation requires special skills. Once learned, they can become spontaneous; you will be able to use them freely and naturally, and in so doing, you will become a more effective encourager.

Ordinarily, one would risk confronting only a dear friend. To confront without a solid relationship would probably be destructive.

Confronting cross-culturally is a special problem, and should be treated with great care. Sensitivity to customs, normal patterns of conversation and special factors in interpersonal relationships need to be carefully undestood before this type of confrontation can be used.

On the other hand, some cultures are very confrontive, and require constant confrontation to be effective. The softer, non-directive approach may be considered as evidence of weakness or insecurity. Your own awareness must be the deciding factor if and when to confront.

It is possible to confront without causing defensiveness in the one you are confronting. One way is to begin by affirming his strengths and then inviting him to examine the problem area you wish to confront. Perhaps the problem area, if dealt with effectively, is one that could be developed into a strength.

A helpful ground rule is to encourage your friend, before he answers your confrontation, to reflect back what he has heard you say. Then if he has misunderstood you, the matter can be cleared up. Once he has understood your confrontation, the two of you can explore the area of weakness or strength more completely. In this way, confrontation becomes a constructive and healing exercise.

Timing Confrontations

Knowing when you have reached the point when you may confront the other person is not always easy. Each stage of your interaction is a source of clarification and discovery. Any reactions either of you have can lead to better understanding and pave the way for more direct helping.

Just as a seeker will test to see if you are really the kind of person he can trust, so you must test out your relationship with him through a minor confrontation. If he can accept and work with your confrontation, you know you can move along. If he is defensive, instead of pursuing the confrontation, you should help him explore his defensiveness and discover why he is reacting that way.

What to Confront

Maladaptive Behavior

Someone has said that dealing with a problem is similar to putting a letter in a mailbox. If you have two hands free, it's easy. If you are loaded down with packages, attempting to put the letter in the slot may cause you to drop a package. Trying to catch that package before it hits the muddy ground causes another to fall. Soon the simple task has become monumental, resulting in frustration and damage.

In a similar way, maladaptive behavior diverts energy into ineffective activity. When a seeker is unable to meet even the simple demands of life, he will turn to others for strength. You can learn how to help him by observing his patterns of action. Your own activity and energy in conversation and approach to problem solving become part of the encouraging process.

As you note the manner in which a person approaches and takes responsibility in solving problems, the way he carries himself and how he responds to you, you will develop hunches about his level of physical and psychological energy.

If he is active, talks of doing many things, and shows interest in a wide variety of subjects, you may assume he has a high energy level. You will probably be able to help him solve his problem quickly. If he is not energetic and active, he may suffer from a physical or psychological disturbance. Each conflict drains energy from the seeker. His strength is sapped by inadequate solutions to his life's problems. As a result, each task seems insurmountable.

Inconsistencies

A seeker's stated feelings and the way he behaves often

are not congruent. Jesus pointed out the Samaritan woman's inconsistency rather quickly. She talked about wanting "living water," and he replied, "Go get your husband." She thus had to admit the inconsistency between her life and her speech. As facilitator, you may not be able to be so direct. But you should be alert to inconsistencies and make them a part of the picture you are forming of the other even if you do not mention them.

Inconsistencies are often found in the way a person talks about doing things as opposed to his actual accomplishments. He may make exaggerated promises but do little about behavior change. He may agree with you and say he's going to do something, but the next time you meet he will have an excuse for not having done it, or, worse, he will try to cover his failure by lying.

Often it is necessary to have feedback from others to discover inconsistencies. With the seeker's permission, parents, siblings, or spouse may be consulted. Often it is helpful to talk to the whole family together. If the seeker balks at this, it may be that he doesn't want his inconsistencies exposed.

The reason for trying to uncover a person's inconsistency is not to judge him but to help him toward deeper, more realistic self-understanding. Awareness of his inconsistencies can provide the needed basis for developing more consistent and congruent behavior.

As the person becomes more aware that you recognize his inconsistencies without condemning him for them, he can examine his reasons for inconsistent behavior. He may discover that his behavior is partly a function of his environment, and partly a function of his inadequate relationships with others and with himself.

Everyone wants his thoughts, feelings, and behavior to be consistent and congruent. The person you are helping is no exception. He wants to be able to be himself in more realistic ways, so that when he acts, he can act consistently with his inner image of himself. When he is consistent, he is free to act without constantly having to rationalize, explain, or justify himself.

In a later chapter we will study plans of action for change in more detail. For the moment, it is enough to learn to help the person develop greater awareness of himself as he is. Motivation to do something about his problems will grow out of that awareness. Awareness and readiness to change are necessary prerequisites to the kinds of behavioral changes that will truly reflect the person's feelings and thoughts and will let him be himself.

Nick

A young minister, Nick, came to me for help because he felt the other counselors had the same hang-ups that he had, and he wanted something different. Nick was an accomplished counselor himself and had worked in a community health center, a hospital, and in prisons as a psychotherapist.

In some ways Nick was a threat to me. He had had much broader experience, in settings that I had not been involved in at all. However, he had known me for some time, so I was reassured.

As we started, it occurred to me that I should listen and respond to the feelings engendered in me by his comments. In doing so, I began to feel into what he was saying and to respond empathically. As he talked, I disclosed my own feelings. Nick would accept, reject or put them "on hold."

He talked about his vocation as a minister and about how his contacts with other ministers seemed pompous and shallow.

I began to wonder if Nick was encountering problems of the same sort within himself. Perhaps he needed to understand his inconsistency. He rejected the idea, but later he came back to it and decided that maybe there was something to it after all. I had anticipated his readiness to change, but he didn't accept the idea until he was ready!

Nick spoke of having "shocked" a ministerial group by swearing in a speech at a convention. I had to *come alive* to that revelation. My feeling was that it had been an attention-getting device, and probably inappropriate.

When I said so, he became angry, but later he said, "I was acting like a rebellious adolescent."

He talked about many other things—about his own confused feelings. I paraphrased those ideas, and he began to perceive himself better. My reflecting his ideas and expressing my own reactions formed the basis of our interchange. Nick was encouraged by the fact that another took him seriously, matching his thoughts and the way he talked. As he was encouraged to move ahead, learning was facilitated, and I understood him better and he began to understand himself more realistically.

Methods of Confrontation

Pairing

Sometimes confrontation takes the form of pinpointing the causes of feelings. When you help a person label his feelings and make a connection between those feelings and a possible cause, you are *pairing*, finding a reason for the feelings. In pairing, you develop hypotheses about the reasons for a person's feelings. The more correct your hypothesis, the better. Sometimes your hypothesis can be judged as more likely to be right if the seeker rejects it. It may be that he or she is not ready for it as was true with Nick. One therapist has said that if your client agrees with you, you are probably wrong. If he disagrees, you are probably right!

If you discover that you really are wrong, though, don't be disheartened. Your warmth and permissiveness will allow the person to correct you and may clarify understanding for both of you. When you accept corrections, the seeker gains confidence in himself and in you. This is especially true in cross-cultural activity.

The more aware the seeker becomes of his feelings and the reasons for them, the better contact he has with reality. As he pairs, he is getting ready to put into action the insights he has acquired, and you are the encourager who has helped bring him to this point.

Pairing requires capturing the essence or central meaning that the seeker is trying to communicate. One response style that can be useful in pairing is to use a word or two to describe the feeling and then state the reason behind the feeling. For example: "You're (sad/happy/disturbed/irritated) (due to/because of/on account of)—" Be careful, however, not to fall into the trap of saying, "You feel—" before each statement. Such repetition seems mechanical and can be irritating.

> *Jane:* I'm very upset. My baby girl is growing up. She doesn't need me as she used to.
>
> *Facilitator:* You're unhappy because your daughter doesn't depend on you as she did.

Practice finding "feeling words" that apply to the person as he is telling you his problem. When both you and the seeker understand and verbalize the essence of his feeling, the whole scope of what he is saying becomes more meaningful.

Pairing Multiples

It is relatively easy to pair a single feeling with a single possible cause. The next step is to help the individual discover multiple causes for multiple feelings, bringing him to a better understanding of the more complicated reality of himself.

For example, Jane may feel lost, sad, or anxious because her growing child is becoming independent. But the actual reason for her complicated feeling may be her fear that her main value to her husband lies in her ability to care for the child. With the child's independence, there may be no reason for her marriage. When a person seems to have more intense feelings than his own explanation supports, it is likely that there are more reasons behind the feelings.

You might say, "You say you're upset because your child is becoming independent. But you're feeling so bad, it seems to me there must be more to it than that. Does her independence perhaps affect your relationship with your husband, and yourself, too?" Or, "Is the child the only reason for your unhappiness?" Or, "Perhaps we should explore other reasons why you are feeling so upset."

Pairing multiple feelings with multiple causes helps the seeker understand himself better, trust you more, look for deeper and more complex reasons for his feelings, and take action on the basis of his new understanding. This is important. Insight is of little value without behavioral change.

Summarizing

From time to time during your interactions with your seeker, summarize the information he has given you and tell him your conclusions about where you feel he is. Your summary may include content and feelings, tying together many elements that have been only briefly touched on and that may at times have seemed unrelated.

Sometimes a person will jump from one subject to another without allowing you to get enough information to know him. In that case your summary might be a reflection that he seems to be skimming the surface of many things and an invitation to go into one subject in more detail. Or you may just review the highlights. Sometimes you might ask him to summarize, saying, "Why don't you review what we have covered so far. Then I'll add to your ideas what I see." Gently make him aware of his need to focus on significant areas.

Usually the summary is used to show a person that he has explored several issues, which gives him the feeling that he is progressing in learning to understand himself. In addition, he will be reassured that you have been listening and helping him fit the pieces together.

Summarizing the previous interview at the beginning of a session helps him appreciate the value of his disclosures. Some feel this procedure is too directive, funneling the person back to previous material. This can be true. However, in a warm and permissive relationship, your friend should feel free to say, "I've covered all that and now I want to move on." But he might appreciate the review and say, "I've thought a lot about one point we talked about. I think I need to investigate it more completely."

Let's see how summarizing can be used effectively in confrontation. Jane has talked about feeling sad because her child is becoming independent. She has also questioned her value as a person to her husband. In other words, she is confused about her genuine worth, apart from her value as a mother.

Jane's real need is to become aware of herself as a person of importance and to realize that she accomplishes what she does *because* she is worthy, not vice versa.

You can summarize the things she has said like this: "You've talked about being sad because your child is becoming independent, and you've also questioned whether your main value to your husband is as a mother, not as a person. This seems to call into question your perception of your personal worth—that you are of value because of what you *do* rather than being valuable because of who you *are*. Does that pretty much sum up what you have been saying?"

Jane can then either partially or fully acknowledge your interpretation, saying, "No, that's only half of it," or "You've covered some important points, but—" or "I do feel I have *some* value, so its not quite that definite," or, "You certainly summarized how I feel. Now—"

Moving Toward Action

All of the helping techniques we have discussed have focused on understanding aimed toward behavioral change or appropriate action. The seeker's self-exploration is facilitated when you break free of your own prejudices or closed-mindedness.

As you enter into the frame of reference of another, you enhance your own perceptions and, more important, you help him know himself.

When the seeker signals to you in any way that he is ready to begin acting on his insights, it is time to help him initiate action.

Some believe that this beginning to act is a special phase, occurring at the end of the helping process. But it will not come about unless it is subtly encouraged from the beginning of the relationship, just as a young child is encouraged to act for himself from the beginning of his development. Each effort toward change should be rewarded. Then, by the time you reach action stage, your friend will already have experimented and taken some responsibility for acting on his understanding.

Action and behavioral change are the goals of the helping process. Empathy and acceptance can lead to insight and understanding, but until these are acted upon and behavioral change results, the procedure is incomplete.

Ted

Ted, a young minister, was distraught. He was on the verge of being dismissed from his job, largely because he couldn't get along with his senior pastor. I came alive to his needs as he talked. He knew he reacted negatively to direction from the pastor, but didn't know why. If he was in on the planning of assignments, though, he didn't react so negatively.

His negative reactions were affecting his home life, as well. He would come home and vent his anger on his wife, children, pets, or anyone else who happened to be around. So Ted was anxious to learn how to accept the direct suggestions that were given to him without becoming angry, negative, and resistant.

As we talked about the problem, a hypothesis began forming. Ted's past relationship with some significant person had preconditioned this response in him. He felt frustrated now because he didn't know the causes of his resentment toward the pastor.

The first step was to understand Ted's feelings. He was angry at the "unfeeling senior pastor," but he was also angry at himself, although he didn't realize it. His preoccupation with the pastor blocked that awareness. "If *he* would change, my life would be fine."

I needed then to lead him indirectly into a consideration of other possibilities. I did so with an open-ended question: "How did you get along with your dad and mother?"

A dam broke. Ted talked on and on about how his father had mistreated him. Ted couldn't do anything right. If he did something well, there was always a way that could have been better. If he got a *B* in school, he should have made an *A*.

As we zeroed in on the past frustration and anger which was recreated in the present, Ted was encouraged to find out what was going on in his relationship with the senior pastor. As I confronted him with what had gone on with his father, he began to make connections between his past difficulties and his present ones.

As we summarized details from his past and he related them to his present problems, he began to see that his feelings of rejection by his father were being transferred to his relationship with his senior pastor. Realizing that, he began to see his associate as a person different from his father. He commented, "What I am doing is reacting to my pastor as if he were my father. No wonder I get so angry when he tells me to do something! All the frustration and irritation of the past boils up within me, and I react the way I had learned to react to my father out of that frustration. I'm not seeing my boss as he is but as I have recreated him in the image of my dad!"

Often the emotions entailed in a past experience are triggered in the present by some element common to the original disturbing experience. With Ted, that element was a man in authority. Each time a man exerted authority over Ted, it was like pushing a button labeled: "Get angry. Someone is pushing you around. Someone is rejecting you."

As Ted understood the reasons for his feelings, he was encouraged to take action to eliminate the automatic responses he was making. Together we reviewed and summarized. Gradually a new picture of his senior pastor began to emerge. He wasn't like Ted's father. He often expressed appreciation for what Ted did, and he was not trying to dominate him.

Ted began to recognize that the senior pastor was not the only one he had put in the position of his father. As he reviewed his experiences, he was able to make appropriate changes in his attitude and behavior toward others as well.

Check Yourself

- If one is to confront effectively, he must be open to confrontation himself. Invite a trusted friend to give you feedback on any maladaptive behaviors or inconsistencies you may have. Accept his feedback and seek to understand the roots of those behaviors and inconsistencies. Understanding your own problems will help you to better understand what another is going through in dealing with his problems.

- When appropriate in a conversation, express your convictions and outlook on life, especially if they differ from the other person's. Invite his feedback on your style of confrontation.

- Find a friend who is willing to share a problem with you, and practice exploring possible causes for the feelings he has. Can you pair feelings with causes? Can you summarize his situation in such a way that his understanding is enhanced?

7

Putting Your
Insights Into Action

Herb, a young minister, was very angry. A trustee seemed
to be standing in the way of his getting what he considered
to be a much needed and deserved pay raise. Although
funds were available, it seemed that this trustee, who had
considerable influence with the board, would rather spend
the money on an addition to the building, which was not a
pressing need. Herb blew his top at him, venting the pent-up
frustration of months of economizing and scraping just to get
by. Later, he thought about his irresponsible outburst and felt
ashamed. He would have to go to the trustee and make
things right.

The next day, Herb's young daughter did something she
had been told not to do. He exploded with fury, far out of
proportion to the girl's misdeed. He scolded her unmercifully,
and she ran crying to her room. Again Herb realized he had
overreacted. He felt terrible as he went to her to apologize.

Herb never had agreed with his in-laws' theology. They
were kind and helpful, but Herb often argued with them.
One day while visiting them, Herb became so irritated that

he couldn't handle it. He exploded, told his wife to get the children's coats, and herded the family out in a huff.

Herb began to realize that his explosions were too extreme. Worse, they were coming at shorter and shorter intervals. He knew he had to do something or he would lose all his friends and eventually his job. He finally came for help.

After a brief review of his situation, we decided to do a behavior analysis. Herb was to write out, in detail, a description of each explosive incident that occurred: what he had been doing beforehand, what he was thinking about, what he said, what the other person said, what actually triggered the blow-up.

The next time he came in, he had catalogued 10 incidents in which he had vented his anger. The very process of recording the incidents had begun to have a positive effect on his behavior. He was forced to remember that in order to get his ideas expressed properly and usefully, he must maintain control.

Writing about his bursts of anger was in inself an analysis of cause and effect for Herb. He began to identify his irresponsible behavior, and he set a specific goal to try to recognize and then deal effectively with the incidents that triggered his anger.

We talked about some of the roots of his difficulty, especially in regard to his father, who, Herb felt, had never responded positively to his ideas. He had to recognize that the people he was now getting angry at were not his father and that they were people whom God loved. He carefully reviewed important parts of his past.

As Herb learned about the roots of his anger, he also learned new ways to deal with it in his present relationships. In so doing, he took responsibility for his own life. He was beginning to learn that anger itself may not be wrong (as Paul said, "Be ye angry, and sin not" [Ephesians 4:26]), but the way he used his anger was wrong.

Using Insights

You, as facilitator, should remind yourself constantly that the reason for a person's seeking you is his unhappiness with his present state. In other words, he wants to *change*. He wants help in exploring his problems and in gaining insight into his behavior and wants to use those insights to grow. He needs an encourager.

In John 3 we read that Nicodemus came to Jesus by night with a need. Perhaps he had been too busy to seek him during the day, or perhaps he did not want anyone to know about his visit. In any case, he was a man who, even though he was successful and respected, intuitively felt something lacking in his life and who wanted to investigate the possibilities of changing. He had enough insight to know that there was more to life than what he had been experiencing.

Jesus dealt with the problem immediately. He knew that Nicodemus was concerned about his needs and was ready to confront them. Because of Jesus' reputation, it may not have taken him a long time to develop rapport, as it usually does. Nicodemus knew his facilitator and was certain that Jesus had something he wanted and needed. He had a desire for knowledge, understanding, and action before he sought Jesus, so they could move quickly on in their program.

You will have to take more time to develop the relationship before achieving the same level of trust. The techniques presented in this book can be thought of as means to the end of helping the person do something about his needs of openness to explore and try out. But, we must always beware that these means do not become ends in themselves—that the process of developing a relationship does not become so comfortable that the seeker's desire to change diminishes or that you, the facilitator, forget the real reason for the contact. This may seem improbable, but in practice it can occur. Continually check to make sure you are both working toward the goal of change.

Choosing Growth

The less you know about a person, the more alternatives for action you might consider. Conversely, the better you know a person, the more alternatives you will eliminate as inappropriate. But although your options will become fewer, they will be more practicable, because they will be suited to his personality and abilities. Your friend has a unique combination of characteristics, and usually only one or a few choices of action will meet his needs and achieve his goal.

Behind each decision the seeker makes is a more basic one: whether to grow in maturity or to remain the same, which may be equivalent to deteriorating. It is a decision for or against growth. The rich young ruler who came to Jesus for help but then turned away made a no-growth decision. He decided to reject the growth experience because he was not willing to give up the one thing that blocked growth for him—preoccupation with the material aspects of life.

Your job as facilitator is to help the person become aware that as he chooses a particular course of action he is also choosing to live either a fuller life or a more restricted one. As you help him formulate problem-solving behavior, you also help him see the ultimate consequences of that behavior. You help him see the implications of growing or not growing as you help him eliminate inappropriate courses of action and choose those that will help him develop the most fully. As you do this, the caring in your relationship also grows, and he is encouraged.

Growth is the development of skills and relationships that draw one closer to what he wants and needs to become. There are two schools of thought regarding the Christian's responsibility to grow. One says, "Be passive and God will change you." The other says, "You have to be active. A ship can't be steered unless it is moving." Paul seems to endorse the latter school when he writes, "Work out your own salvation" (Phil. 2:12).

Jesus, likewise, encourages our initiative aided by his direction and strength. It is interesting that in his contacts with people, Jesus usually prescribed patterns of action that were aimed at ultimate growth. "Abundant life," "Go and sin no more," "The water I give is everlasting," "Sell what you have and give to the poor," "Be born again" are all expressions of his concern for our growth. Review carefully the settings in which those statements were made in order to understand them fully. Jesus encouraged action toward growth in spiritual experience. He did not subscribe to the model, too often endorsed today, that waits for God to engineer our every action and thought.

Just as God does not necessarily direct each small choice we make, so you as the facilitator cannot become the sole director of another's action. But you can become a stimulus for growth. Jesus is our ultimate pattern for development, but he leaves the responsibility for the details to us.

Setting Action Goals

Insights are encouraging, but in order to be truly helpful, they need to be translated into specific goals for action. For example, your friend, as a Christian, may have set "following God's will" as his goal. That is an excellent long-range goal, but it is not defined clearly enough to act on it.

Effective goals have certain prerequisites. Keep in mind the following principles when outlining an action program:

1. A goal must be strongly desired and be consistent with a person's needs.
2. You and your friend must be convinced of the worth of the goal and be willing to work to achieve it.
3. The goal must specify certain behaviors and be attainable.
4. Progress toward the goal must be observable and measurable. (For example, if you can count the times a desired behavior action occurs, progress is measurable.)

The general goal of following God's will meets criterias 1

and 2, but not 3 and 4. A more specific action goal related to that general desire might be, "I want to stop talking negatively about other people." That goal fulfills all the above criteria. Both of you are convinced of its value. It is attainable. The person can count the number of times he gossips about others each day and, at the end of each day, can record that data on a frequency chart to see whether he is improving day by day.

How to Define Goals

Your friend may have expressed his problem in general terms such as, "I'm depressed—I'm frustrated—I'm lonely." Your empathic responses can help him become more descriptive, allowing you to help him define the problem, using the information he gives you.

Still being understanding and tactful, you can then help him to be specific regarding what he would like to have changed, asking an action-oriented question such as, "What can you do about your problem?" For example, Jane comes to you saying, "People don't like me." An action question such as, "What could you do to make yourself more attractive to others?" might help her discover and initiate a specific course of action.

Such questions help people think beyond their own unhappiness. Each suggestion or question should help the person, in small positive steps, find a way out of his difficulty. Others say, "Just do." You say, "Think of some specific actions that will help achieve your goal."

Some say, "Pray," implying that the seeker has *not* prayed or is ineffective in his prayers. Unfortunately, many people have been desperately praying for years about their problem and still need help. Maybe that's why they have sought you. You can help them give feet to their prayers so that positive action will result.

Perhaps your seeker's problem is that he compares himself

negatively with others. He is never satisfied with his own performance because he knows someone who does better. He may try to live up to an ideal composed of the best traits of many people. The impossibility of his goal sets the stage for constant failure.

In this case, your action goal may be to realistically clarify and assess the characteristics of the idealized model and help your seeker get accurate feedback on his strengths. Gaining new understanding and a more accurate self-image, he can then deal with his frustration more realistically and develop a plan to cope with his problems.

Perhaps your seeker seems to have no goal at all. He may regard his life as purposeless, without meaning. Helping him become aware of his need for goals will be the first step toward improvement. Getting him actively involved is essential, for meaning in life is directly related to progress toward defined goals. Your understanding of the Christian faith and its practical outworking can encourage him to set up meaningful goals. You can become a model, by your lifestyle, attitudes, and behavior, of what it is to live purposefully. However, you must not manipulate your friend. He must be willingly involved in the whole process of goal setting.

Be specific, not general, in your example and discussion. Exactly how has your faith helped you solve specific problems or formulate goals? Can you define and clarify your own action goals? If not, it would be better to remain silent about them. You will need to do some soul searching before being able to offer such help to your friend.

We all need a purpose in life. It can be provided by the conviction that there is a God who values us, is concerned about us, and has a place for us. Unfortunately, much religious teaching does little to translate this knowledge of self-worth into constructive, active living. You, the facilitator, may provide meaningful encouragement to your friend by helping him define and clarify action goals.

Appropriateness of Goals

Helping another set goals demands many of the same techniques as do paraphrasing, clarifying, and identifying feelings and facts. Verbalized goals require clarification and checking for appropriateness.

At times the action goal chosen by your seeker may turn out to be inappropriate—impossible to attain or against his best interest. If so, you may find yourself in a real quandary. You want to help a person become more independent, yet telling him what to do may have exactly the reverse effect.

Remember, as in any social relationship, you may give opinions about potential courses of action. Perhaps you have been through a similar situation and can therefore use your own experience as testimony. Or you might raise questions about the potential results of a particular action. Or the seeker himself may request your opinion. In any case, it is important that he himself take responsibility for making the final decision about a course of action. If you let him trap you into deciding what he is to do, it will be your "fault" if it doesn't work. Always shift the responsibility back to the seeker.

Sometimes it is difficult to define goals and a course of action. Your seeker may say, "I can't get along with other people, and I don't know why." In such a case, he will have to analyze his behavior. You may suggest that he notice and record those actions that seem to affect relationships adversely. If a broader perspective is needed, a spouse or parent can add to the observations, thus providing you with even more objective information. Reviewing such information, you can help him start to pinpoint areas needing change and to define goals in line with his needs.

Timing of Goal Setting

If you talk about goals permaturely, before you have properly established a trusting relationship that encourages growth and personal responsibility, your friend may feel manipulated or acted upon instead of feeling a part of the action. If that happens, he may give up, resist, or feel criticized.

In everyday life, goals are often not verbalized or identified as such. Therefore, you might not want at first to use the word *goal* in your discussion but to ask, instead, something like, "In what direction do you think you should go in order to become more effective/see things differently/become more acceptable?" Those are goals, but you have not labled them as such.

When you unobtrusively give a person direction, it may seem so natural to him that he may think it was his own idea. He will feel hopeful and encouraged and be largely unaware of the sequence of problem, goal, action, and relief that he is going through. He gains confidence in himself and the future and, as he reaches his goals, he feels capable of being self-directing.

A happy by-product is that as your friend changes and grows, you change also. This reciprocal development continues and becomes self-energizing as you participate actively in the relationship.

Axel's Depression

Difficulties and frustrations seemed to get Axel down more quickly and for a longer time than they did other people. He constantly reviewed his problem He decided to do something about the problem. In counseling, he began to reconstruct experiences from the past that related to the problem. He carefully reviewed the circumstances, and especially his thoughts about them, that often led to his depression. He reviewed what actually happened, who was involved, and the elements common to each situation. The Spirit of God was present in this analysis, working through his therapy and his thinking.

Axel's behavioral analysis clarified several problem areas. He recognized connections he had not been aware of before. One element common to all his depressive episodes was the unrealistic expectations that he had for himself and for others. He set impossible goals for himself, and when he failed to reach them, he felt inadequate and frustrated. That led him to feeling worthless and depressed. Then, because he had failed to reach his impossible goals, he played the "Axel is a failure" role.

Axel began to realize that the source of the problem was not that depression caused him to fail to reach his goals, but that his style of goal setting itself was the source of his depression. He constantly set himself up for failure by expecting more of himself than he could deliver. He did the same to others, as well; in a sense, he set goals for them. When they didn't fulfill his expectations in their relating to him, he became depressed. When neither his expectations of himself nor his expectations of others were met, as they seldom were, the effect was disastrous.

Through analyzing these cause-and-effect relationships, Axel began to learn how to avoid the traps he set for himself. He learned to be reasonable in his expectations and to set goals that were consistent with his needs and abilities.

Ambivalence in Goals

As the person accumulates information in his behavior analysis he may discover that he wants two goals that are incompatible with each other. He is attracted to both, but in gaining one, will lose the other. For example, he may want total independence but he also likes to be married. In the face of such ambivalence, clarifying goals requires painstaking effort in analysis and careful weighing of consequences. A similar difficulty arises when a person wants to achieve socially unacceptable goals.

Some people do not seem to be truly interested in achieving goals. You will have to decide whether you want to spend time with a person who has no clear direction or who seems to want none. If you are willing to take the time, suggesting a careful log of activities may be the start of such a person's behavioral analysis.

The person who has no goal may not be wanting to look at himself analytically. Having no goal is his protection against facing himself realistically. With careful intervention, you may be able to penetrate that facade. Convinced of your good will, he may begin to explore some hidden dissatisfactions within himself, and, in so doing, he may gradually translate his problems into goals in spite of his ambivalent feelings about himself and his life.

Modeling as Direction

The life Christ lived with his disciples gave them a model for their development. For example, he washed their feet (John 13:15) as a model of servanthood. Watching how he did things, his disciples learned to plan action for themselves after he returned to heaven. Listening to him speak, raise questions, and establish goals, they learned to plan their own actions more meaningfully.

You likewise can be a model. Your manner of accumulating data, analyzing behavior, looking at alternative courses of action, and helping a person choose and actualize his goals become procedural models for learning.

As you work with a person, he will gain helpful knowledge not only from the information you give but also from watching the ways you help him attack his problems. This encourages him to transfer new skills to other situations without becoming dependent on you. As he sees the results, he becomes motivated to try harder.

Remember, your ultimate goal is not just to meet immediate needs but to make the seeker self-determining by teaching him *how* to handle problems. Then, when he is not with you, he will be able to cope with new situations or painful feelings on his own.

Goals and Relationships

Drawing goals from a person's problems is just one way to develop action goals. It often involves confrontation, as when Jesus said to the Samaritan woman, "Call your husband." With that single comment, he pinpointed the basic problem in her life—that of relationship. We don't have the details of how Jesus worked out a behavioral change plan for her, but they must have discussed some specific plan of action in addition to her being reborn.

Frequently a person who comes to you for help with a relationship may not be the only one who needs the help. For example, his difficulty may actually be a family problem. To set action goals for the seeker alone may not be entirely effective. Instead, the whole family needs to be involved before helpful action can be planned.

When a group confrontation is not feasible, however, even helping one person in the family might be a catalyst for changing the behavior of others in the family. You might say: "Let's analyze how I might help you deal more effectively with your (wife, child, relative, boss, fellow worker) so you can help him, if he is willing, to change his behavior." If one person in a relationship changes, the other has to change, since he cannot respond in his habitual way to someone who now reacts differently. Each person, then, has the potential to promote change in others. One wife who came to talk, even though her husband wouldn't, changed so much that her husband began to change. Then he wanted to come, too, to find out what was going on!

Being Accountable

Accountability means taking stock of your and the other person's progress toward the goals—openness, sharing, and behavior change—that the two of you set up. You are both accountable in determining the process of your helping interviews, the goals to be achieved, and the solutions to be implemented. At the beginning of the helping process, you may take more initiative in order to move the person toward change. Gradually, though, you must transfer that initiative to him by checking on how he is carrying out the program the two of you have set up. Urge him to take more responsibility for proposing new ways to accomplish his goals.

Helping a person change his behaviors usually involves teaching him new skills to replace his old, counterproductive ones. You, as well as the other person are accountable for the progress he makes in learning those skills.

Another area of accountability must be stressed. As a Christian facilitator, you also are accountable to God. The Spirit of God can help you as you try to help another, but you must maintain the proper balance between expecting God to do everything and your taking whole responsibility for yourself.

The Spirit of God, facilitates the counseling process, motivating, clarifying, and energizing you in directions that may seem obscure or impossible. The love of God working through you helps you maintain an attitude of concern for the worth and value of others. That in itself is encouraging.

Sometimes helpers say, in effect, "God, make me a channel through which your Spirit can work—but don't change me!" This attitude has two flaws. First, both you and the seeker must grow in the relationship—which means you will change. Second, God has to use us—our personalities and lives—to achieve his purpose, and so he honors efforts to become more skilled. Both hard work and inspiration are necessary and will result in change in you as well as in those you help. Be open to that!

Prayer helps you see things from a different perspective. It is not a retreat or withdrawal from service, nor does it require a formal break in conversation. It is the continual, on-going breathing to God that can become part and parcel of all your activity. As Jesus said, "Pray without ceasing." Prayer can give you continuing insight and encouragement to realistically face the difficulties you are working through with another.

Accountability recognizes the balance between what you personally must do for others, and what God can do through you and through the initiative of the person whom you are helping.

Helen

Helen came for counseling to learn the reasons behind her inability to manage her little girl.

The first thing I told her to do was to make a behavior analysis of each day's experiences to help define the problem. This record became the means for helping her to recognize what was going on and to discover causes for the problems she was experiencing. Helen accepted accountability for changing and, through prayer and Bible study, was helped by the Spirit of God. As she faithfully recorded her activities and responses to the various causes of her behavior, she began to realize that the behavior that had seemed unexplainable before was becoming understandable, and she began to identify cause/effect relationships.

As the reasons for her behavior became clear, she began to want to do something about them in order to change. Insight was encouraging, but it wasn't enough. She wanted to *change.*

The first goal she set for herself was to begin to respond with patience to her daughter, who was active and resistant to direction. The girl's disobedience caused Helen to become upset and react in unhelpful ways, which exacerbated the problem. It had become a contest of wills.

The goal of showing patience specified responding kindly

but firmly to the child. Helen made a chart, and each time she reacted patiently, she gave herself a check. At first responding patiently was difficult, but as she became more aware of what triggered her impatience, she began to improve. She felt rewarded when she was able to give herself a check on the chart and was disappointed ("punished") when she failed.

After the first week, her improvement was rapid. Her child began to respond differently to her and her husband noticed a change in her attitude toward him, as well. Helen became able to translate the love of God within her into an observable fruit of the Spirit—*patience.*

Causes and Effects

As we evaluate our accountability, we sometimes forget that for every effect, there is a cause. Sometimes the cause is forgotten and needs to be brought to memory. Other times a special program to clarify cause-and-effect relationships is required.

One problem common to many churches is their failure to relate causes and goals. When someone joins a church or accepts Christ, we encourage him to study the Bible and then assume that he will automatically change his lifestyle. Lives of failure, frustration, and apparent unhappiness in our churches, however, indicate that those expectations are not necessarily valid.

We need to specifically define behavioral objectives. We can set up contingency (cause-and-effect) programs to aid people make changes in their behavioral patterns. In contingency management, we define goals and constantly check on progress toward them. Rewards or punishment reinforce the desired behavior. This behavior-modification approach can be used by God's Spirit through you in a warm, accepting, and encouraging atmosphere, to accomplish his purpose. It must not be mechanical brainwashing or simply humanistic. Rather, defining relationships between specific causes and effects in the seeker's life, rewarding desired behaviors, and punishing undesirable behavior give you concrete means by which you can encourage more effective behaviors in your life and in the life of the one whom you are helping.

The best way to be an ENCOURAGER is to follow the pattern that Jesus followed in discipling. Barnabas must have done the same with Mark to prepare him to return to duty.

Tim

Tim was completely discouraged. He began to make plans to leave the mission field and return to the States, defeated. As he was getting ready to mail his letter of resignation to the mission board and was beginning to pack, his thoughts turned to memories of his time of pre-field training at the Link Care Center.

As he reviewed the skills he had been taught and the ideas and patterns that he had learned there, new ways of approaching his present problems started to come to him. In training he had had several individual sessions with a counselor in which they had worked out ways to analyze problems.

Instead of finishing his packing, he began to keep a record of his actions and thoughts. He began to see that he had not set up observable and measurable goals, only general, nonspecific ones. Tim decided to try to define, clarify, and check the appropriateness of the goals he had chosen on the field. He began to recognize some of the ambivalence he felt about his work and to sort out some of his true feelings.

He recalled his ultimate model, Jesus Christ, and the model of the person he had talked with back home. Those models helped him to redefine and clarify his direction and put new plans into action. Many fruitful years of mission work resulted.

Check Yourself

- Set a goal for yourself in relation to a problem you are currently having. Do you strongly desire that goal? Are you convinced it is worth the effort it will take to reach it? Does it specify certain behaviors? Is it observable and measurable? Setting goals for yourself will give you a feel for what is involved in helping another choose and set goals.

- Help a seeker to set action goals in relation to a problem he is having. Examine with him whether his goals are appropriate and attainable. Check to see if there is any ambivalence in his goals.

- Pray about the goals you and your seeker have set. Remember that your primary accountability, as a Christian, is to God.

8

The Results
May Surprise You

"One thing I don't understand," Ann said. "Before I came to see you I had a lot of things bothering me. I reacted negatively to things that weren't really important. I was angry much of the time. I reacted without thinking.

"Now, those things that bothered me before are no longer a big problem to me. I see them for what they really are— usually just minor adjustments on the way to solving my problems or things to motivate me to make necessary changes. My whole perspective has changed.

"Of course, I slip once in a while and find myself wallowing in self-pity and depression. But even then I can say to myself, 'This too shall pass. I'll do the best that I can in the light of these circumstances, and I'll soon feel better.' And sure enough, it isn't long before the feelings go away. Soon I feel cheerful again.

"But I don't know *how* this all has happened. It's a mystery to me. It seems like we have talked only about common, ordinary things. You responded to me. I looked at the situation and discovered reasons for my feelings. But how did that change things for me?

"I guess the Spirit of God used you as a tool to teach me lessons I wouldn't have learned otherwise. I'm not sure how it happened, but I'm sure grateful it did!"

Ann expressed a feeling common to those who have been encouraged through the means described in this book. Her attitude toward life is different, and she is grateful for it. She recognizes that the Spirit of God can use other people as tools of encouragement for those in need of help.

You, too, can be an instrument of encouragement if you are prepared to discover what you can do. If you have read, practiced, and internalized all of the methods and procedures described in this book, you *are* able to encourage effectively. As you gain more skill, you will have many "Ann's" express their appreciation to God for you.

Usually, however, reflecting feelings, analyzing their causes and setting goals is not enough to solve a problem. Many people need help to act on their insights and achieve their goals. This is particularly true of people struggling with depression. They often feel both hopeless and helpless. When your "Ann" has reached the point of despair, you can assign constructive tasks that will help her become more confident and active in meeting her problems.

Dealing with Depression

Depression is the most common emotional problem in our society today. All of us can get caught up in ruminating on all the negative things that happen or have happened to us. Each new disturbing experience confirms the feeling that everything is bad and won't get any better. We dig ourselves into a deeper and deeper hole, with slippery sides, and we despair of ever getting out.

If your friend is struggling with depression, simple verbal encouragement is of little help. In fact, the more you point out the good things he has to be thankful for, the more depressed he will become, because he will feel that his depression is irrational and blameworthy.

Depression usually results from that kind of circular thought process. If it is not too severe, depression can usually be helped by a direct action program aimed at breaking that circular thought process.

In addition, it is wise to recommend a medical checkup, since physiological problems can cause or contribute to depression.

The following case illustrates how the helping skills presented in this book can be used in dealing with this most common of emotional problems.

Flo was feeling terrible. She woke up each morning feeling as though the weight of the world were on her shoulders. Her whole world had become bleak. If she began to feel better, something always happened to drive her down to the depths again. She began to avoid going out. When people came to the house she would go to a back bedroom, asking her husband to tell the visitor that she wasn't feeling well. She avoided going to her classes and as she fell further behind in her schoolwork, she became even more depressed. Everything she did or didn't do fed into her depressive system.

Flo came for encouragement, and it didn't take long to realize that she was caught up in the web of her thought processes. Logic had given way to illogical thinking. She found imaginary reasons for her depressive thoughts.

The first action task I assigned to her was a direct helping task—to think back and catalogue each time she had felt depressed over the years. She was to describe the surrounding circumstances, where she had been, who else had been involved, and anything else she could remember. The more details she could add, the more helpful it would be.

As she did this, reviewing the details of each depressive

episode in her past, she began to feel worse and worse. She complained that the exercise hadn't helped her at all.

I pointed out that the information she was "mining" out of her past was to become the basis for an action plan for future use. She was "reliving" her past.

That wasn't much reassurance to her, but with considerable urging, she kept on.

Another reason I wanted Flo to do this review was that as she was flooded with the negative emotions of the past, the present would become more attractive. No matter what she had to face today, it would seem better than the things in her past.

Included in Flo's catalogue was a day-by-day account of how she reacted to her present problems. If something troublesome happened, she wrote about it in detail, emphasizing the kind of thoughts she had at the moment. The careful documenting of her thought patterns helped her realize the part she herself was playing in her problems. She began to see the ways that her thoughts led her into self-blaming, self-depreciation, and feelings of depression.

Gathering raw data about the way an individual develops his pattern of thinking is very important. Each of us develops thought patterns that condition the way we act. When something happens, we respond with a habitual thought, which starts the pattern of thinking like a music box, playing its way to the end no matter what. When we develop negative "tunes," each replay becomes longer and increases our depressive thoughts.

Together, Flo and I analyzed the data she had gathered. Childhood experiences had led her to develop thought patterns which were amplified by more recent events. Negative feelings from the past added their weight to her present thinking and feeling, making her even more upset.

One negative pattern Flo had been following would be triggered whenever she made some mistake, or thought she had. That experience would bring up thoughts of self-condemnation from the past. *There you go again—you stupid idiot. You just can't do anything right. You're just repeating the same things the way you did before. Everyone is going to criticize you, and be more aware of how stupid and inept you are. You'll never learn how to be effective.*

Thus a minor error generalized into a total condemnation of everything from the past and present and became a prediction for the future. In the midst of this thought process, she recognized her perfectionistic tendencies and Flo would become so tense and depressed that she would make more mistakes and feel even more inept. The constant repetition of her negative thinking wore her down and left her completely fatigued.

Circular thought processes must be stopped. Awareness of what the thought process is helps and is a necessary first step. Keeping track of the actual thoughts makes a person aware of the pattern so that action can be initiated immediately to cut off the further progression of thoughts.

Several *thought-stopping* procedures can be used. Shouting to oneself, *"Stop! Stop! Stop!"* when negative thoughts begin sometimes helps. Writing the thought on a card also disrupts them. Wearing a rubber band on one's wrist and snapping it enough to hurt when negative thoughts begin is very effective. Whatever method is used, it must be administered immediately when the thought occurs, and it must be used consistently. The negative pattern has been developed and used for years and is highly resistant to change. This re-educational process requires constant repetition over a long period of time to be effective.

Similar to thought-stopping is *thought substitution*. Carrying a number of small cards on which are written select Bible verses or encouraging sayings, which can be taken out and read when negative thoughts begin, can often change the thought pattern. One's thoughts take a new, positive direction and the negative cycle stops.

An encourager cannot emphasize too much the importance of consistent application of these techniques. Each time the old pattern continues without being interrupted by one of these methods, the old pattern is reinforced. Changing thought patterns is hard work, and the depressive feelings themselves, making everything seem hopeless, contribute to the lack of desire to carry out the task. But the results of persistence are worth the effort. You, the encourager, must constantly check and reinforce each little step forward. You are the key to maintaining the motivation to keep on working toward the desired goal.

Flo began to notice a change in her thought patterns as she consistently applied these methods. She began to be alert to the old, negative thoughts as soon as they occurred instead of afterward. For example, if her boss was busy doing other things when she tried to talk to him, the familiar negative began. *See, you're not worth much. He doesn't pay any attention to you. You're of no value.* Immediately, she recognized the pattern and substituted the thought, *My boss is being inconsiderate. He must have a problem. He's awfully busy, but what I have to say is important. If I don't force him to give me attention, he'll be missing an idea necessary for our work.*

That change in her thought pattern, which by now she was able to make quite easily, allowed her to relax and think of a better way to get her boss's attention. When she did so, he responded positively and appreciated her ideas, which rewarded her.

Flo began writing out alternative plans of action whenever she had to deal with a situation she didn't like. Each time she handled a problem situation constructively, she felt stronger. Her reasons for feeling bad began to erode. Each success, though small, became a reason for feeling better.

Assertiveness

Assertiveness is important to growth. Old habits are part of the old nature that Paul writes about (Romans 7:14-23). As Christians, we have the Spirit of God within us, helping

Be assertive–escape from the prison of your own making

us and giving us power to break the hold that the old, sinful nature has on us. The Holy Spirit can use the tools you have been learning to help your seeker break destructive habits.

The continued and regular use of the methods of relearning may help us to obey Jesus' command to take up our cross *daily* (Luke 9:23-27), denying past sinful and unhelpful patterns of life. (It is interesting to note that Luke, the physician, was the only one of the Gospel writers who recorded the word *daily* in that command; it is the key to the whole process.)

Your task as a facilitator is to encourage your seeker by helping him become consistent in the applying the processes whereby the "old man" can be defeated and the "new man" can develop.

Flo was in a difficult spot again. A man she felt she loved had cancelled a date, and she was sure she had lost him. Her thoughts went on: *It's obvious he doesn't like me. He could have arranged his time better so he wouldn't have had to cancel our date. This is just evidence that I'm no good, and he has found it out. This is his way of letting me down easily, and pretty soon he won't call at all. I'm just not the kind of person he wants. I'm of no value.*

Flo had thought herself into deep depression by the time she came for help. Although she could now handle her thoughts at work, a love relationship was so sensitive, she didn't know how to deal with it. The old negative thought patterns reasserted themselves and drove her into despair.

An analysis of what had happened was in order. Gentle questions elicited facts that she had overlooked because her negative thought processes focused only on how bad she was. Negative reasoning had stirred up such a cloud of dusty thinking that the true outline of what had happened was obscured.

"Did he give a reason for breaking the date?"

"Yes. He said an unexpected business appointment came up at work, so he had to follow through on that."

"Is this unusual? That is, has he had to rearrange his appointments with others and with you for that reason at other times?"

"Yes. His job is very demanding, and he is devoted and wants to do his best. That's why he is so successful."

"So you aren't the only one who gets stood up?"

"No. It's even a joke in our crowd. We plan an event, and everyone agrees on the time. Then someone will say, 'That is, if Jack's business appointments don't get in the way.' Then we all laugh about it."

"Did he say he'd call you again?"

"Yes, as soon as he could, and then we'd go out for dinner."

Thus Flo's faulty reasoning was exposed. Encouraged, Flo felt she could go through that exercise herself, asserting her own reasoning, the next time a similar situation arose.

That interchange shows, briefly, how not paying attention to all aspects of an incident can start negative thought patterns. Because Flo was in the habit of blaming herself or her inadequacies for every negative occurance, she would overlook the real reasons behind what happened. Each supposed rejection started her self-condemning thoughts, which reinforced her belief that rejection was caused by her own lack of worth.

As an encourager, you can often help your seeker by going over a problem situation in detail to discover if he has been overlooking something. When a seeker is plagued with self-doubt, you can remind him of the truth that each of us is created in God's image (reading Genesis 1:42, 47; 5:3; 9:6 to him may be helpful). Further, emphasize that God's sending His Son to die for us demonstrates our value. When we accept His Son, we are born into the family of God, which in turn makes us part of a whole worthy structure.

A depressed person forgets those truths. They must be emphasized again and again.

Self-worth

When Flo had reviewed her conversation with Jack and had recognized the negative thought processes that had led her into depression, she began to see that her estimate of her own self-worth needed to be examined. She had been attend-

ing a small group as part of her therapy. One night, the subject of self-esteem came up for discussion, and she noted that many others in the group also had problems with it. As she heard how they were caught in the trap of negative thoughts, she began to see how she had been "taken in."

"If you really had your feelings of self-worth clear, you could stand under a lamp post for the rest of your life, do nothing, and still feel all right about yourself!" The speaker was a young minister. He often introduced prickly subjects in the group to stimulate discussion and, some thought, to avoid dealing with his own problems, so the others in the group immediately responded with disagreement. But when they saw he was very serious, they listened. "Our value doesn't come from what we do. It comes from who we are. We are created by God. There can be no value greater than that. Perhaps, that's why the Bible says, 'Your righteousness is as filthy rags.' God knows the ultimate value each of us has, and he pointed it out that way."

Suddenly everyone was talking at once. Some agreed; some disagreed. Eventually, I was able to bring order to the group so we could hear what each member wanted to say.

Flo said, "Then I don't need to affirm my value by being so busy and trying to make everyone else happy. I don't need to prove myself. I can just be what God has created me to be."

She broke down in tears. Sobs of repentance for her past errors were accompanied by sobs of joy in recognizing God's true view of her. Her negative thoughts had been used by the devil to defeat her and make her feel useless.

Now she could carry on with her activities, but for an entirely different reason. She said, "If what you say is true, and I believe it is, then what I do becomes valuable *because* I'm doing it. I don't get value *from* doing my job or tasks—I *give* value to my job and work. What a difference that makes to me! I feel like that bubbling well of water that Jesus spoke about! I'm ready to do the task. I don't want to stand under the lamp post—I don't need to. I can do my job with joy and thanksgiving!"

Flo was beginning to realize what the truly victorious Christian life was all about. She used to think that "victory" was an absence of hardship, difficulty, problems, or temptations. She now began to realize that the victory came not in avoiding problems but in dealing with them and solving them. She could now thank God for "all things," because even the difficulties could be used in her development and growth (Romans 8:28, 33; Ephesians 5:20). Without a "thorn in the flesh" (2 Corinthians 12:7), which Paul said was to keep one humble, Flo might not become the person God wanted her to become. Difficulties were stimuli to provoke constructive action and promote growth.

Perfectionism and Depression

Flo was discouraged again. It seemed that no matter what she did, it wasn't enough. Others reassured her, but even that didn't help, because she thought they were just trying to make her feel good. No one could really convince her that she was doing well or that others were satisfied with her work. She felt she really pleased no one; she knew she wasn't pleasing herself.

The root of her problem was her image of herself. Because she had feelings of self-depreciation, she brought those feelings to whatever she did, and nothing was acceptable. Believing that she could please anyone was impossible, so she was constantly frustrated.

Her first glimmer of hope had been the realization that much of her problem came from her faulty analysis of her experiences. Then she had begun to accept her own worth as a gift of God. But often, when confronted with her shortcomings, she let her hope be dashed. All she could think about were Jesus' words, drilled into her as a child, "Be ye perfect as your Father in heaven is perfect" (Matthew 5:48).

She could almost hear her mother criticizing her, reminding her of those words. Nothing Flo did could be perfect, so she could never be satisfied, and she drove herself into a state of feeling helpless and hopeless.

Perfectionism is a common cause of depressed feelings, and it is a serious problem. The perfectionist never or seldom feels satisfied with what he has done. Perfectionism often has its roots in the past. Just as negative emotions flood

Perfectionism may lead to depression

back in response to a present reminder of a past experience, so does perfectionism. Any small reminder would start the rehearsal of all of Flo's negative thoughts and feelings from those early criticisms. The effect of that rehearsal, especially as it tied into her religious upbringing, was overwhelming.

Simply reasoning with Flo did little to help. She needed to reeducate herself by thought-stopping whenever self-critical thoughts began, and she needed to analyze those critical thoughts to recognize them as irrational. Analyzing those thoughts, she began to realize that the criticism she felt came from herself, not from others.

Writing out each of her irrational beliefs and expectations helped her to recognize their flaws. Whenever she began to feel depressed, rereading what she had written helped her to think more realistically.

Perfectionistic people are driven by the *musts, shoulds,* and *oughts* of unrealistic expectations. When identified and realistically evaluated, they lose their power to bring depression.

Flo had tried to do a job that really was beyond her training, and she felt she had failed, even though for a beginner she had done well. She sighed, "I know I *should* do better. Other people are able to, and they do better. I *must* succeed

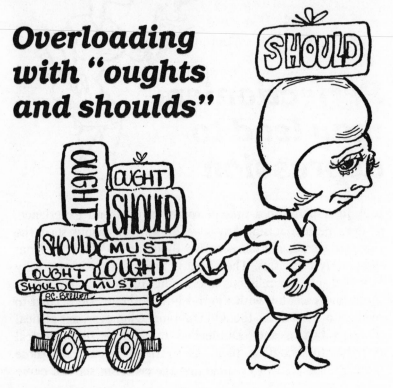

Overloading with "oughts and shoulds"

in this job or I'll be fired." (Other sources revealed that her boss thought she did very good work.)

"I *ought* to get up earlier in the morning and get more reading done. My boss incidently mentions that he gets up at 4:00 A.M. and does his creative work, and I am shattered. I *ought* to do the same. Why can't I do more?" (Her family thinks she is doing a great deal and wishes she would do less.)

"I get migraine headaches, and then I can do nothing. My stomach hurts, and my job doesn't get done. I feel dizzy, and words blur in front of my eyes, and I can't continue reading. What should I do? What should I do?"

Flo's body was telling her to slow down and to become satisfied with less than she was trying to do. But Flo kept trying to do more. She had reached a point where an encourager could help her. She was ready to try something different.

I reviewed with her the peak experience she had had in realizing that her worth was greater than what she did. That memory brought her hope and motivated her to try to deal with her problem of perfectionism.

From her conversation, you can begin to discover the thought processes Flo needed to change. They primarily involved her rating herself and comparing herself to others. She had created an ideal model composed of the best of several different people, and she had tried to be as good as all of them put together. Somehow she had to become aware of how she was thinking.

In a case like Flo's, one of the first things you can do is to have your seeker identify and write out the *musts, oughts* and *shoulds* that drive him. That helps him to see that he is giving himself misinformation about his performance; the criticism isn't coming from others. He must realize that illogical thinking is contributing to his psychological and phys-

ical problems. Further, he alone can change his misery by
learning how to root out and destroy the self-destructive
thoughts and change his attitutes. While you or I may help a
seeker find new ways of facing problems, it must be the
seeker himself who follows through and makes the necessary
changes in behavior and thinking.

"I want you to write out in detail, each one of your negative thoughts about yourself. Think of all the 'shoulds,'
'oughts,' and 'musts' that drive you, and make a list of
them." (Making a list like this is itself a kind of punishment
and thus tends to reduce the frequency of the negative
thought.)

Flo was hesitant. "If I write out a list, it will remind me of
my problems. How can that help? I don't want to do that."

"Do you want to get better, or do you enjoy being the way
you are?"

"Of course I want to get better. That's why I'm here. You
know that."

"It's up to you to make the changes in your thought patterns. No one can do it for you. I can help you get started,
but it's up to you. This method of dealing with your type of
problem has been shown to be effective. Do you want to
work on it or not?"

Flo decided that she did, even though she didn't like it.
Her list was very revealing.

I *should* be the best worker in my office, making fewer
mistakes, typing faster than anyone else, and being the most
efficient person there.

I *ought* to earn my parents' approval because they brought
me into the world and cared for me when I was helpless. If I
don't get their love and assurance that I'm all right, I'll never
be satisfied.

I *must* be competent in everything I try to do. If I'm not,
I can't try anything new because I *ought* not make mistakes.

As Flo reviewed her expectations, her list grew. In fact, it grew so long it became ridiculous, and she began to realize what an impossible life she was trying to live. The very act of identifying and describing her expectations and attitudes helped her gain a clearer perspective and avoid self-punishing thoughts.

In subsequent sessions, Flo examined her irrational expectations. She began to see that she herself was the source of those ideas. She also began to realize that it wasn't necessary to be the best, and that she could encourage others by noticing when they were doing better work than she was. Affirming others became as important to her as her attempts to affirm herself.

"Homework," practicing confronting her negative thinking, was an important supplement to Flo's sessions. An important part of her homework was to keep a journal recording her thoughts and feelings in each problem situation. The messages she told herself were important to note: "I can't do that"; "I'm afraid I'll fail"; "I've got to be perfect"; "What would dad say!"; "I can't stand to be turned down, so I won't ask."

Writing down and analyzing those self-messages showed her her errors. She could see how they prevented her from going ahead with plans and living the way she wanted to. A special assignment of going over each irrational belief for ten minutes a day started the process of weakening its hold on her.

To following up these procedures of recording and analyzing her self-messages, I asked Flo to chart her progress in changing, answering questions like, "What was I thinking this week? Were my thoughts irrational? In what way? How often? When I became aware of negative thinking, what did I do? If it was in connection with a new circumstance, how did I feel? Anxious? Did I override my fears and handle it anyway?"

Shoulds, musts and *oughts* often interfere with the joyful expression of our Christian faith in service to God. Satan can use them to cripple us and make us ineffective in God's service. Flo needed to realize that and to replace her self-condemning, perfectionistic thinking with positive, Christ-centered thinking.

Flo began to feel she was gaining control of her thoughts. She began to see that the Holy Spirit could use her self-monitoring to change her thinking from negative to positive.

But she still felt unsettled. "I really need to plan my life better. How can I learn to be more effective? I waste time being afraid to start. I waste time worrying about what to do. I can't decide on short-term goals. I know my ultimate goal—I want to serve God. But I feel defeated. What can I do?"

Flo needed help to begin acting on her insights. We developed a series of concrete steps, which she could use in a variety of situations, to help her answer her questions.

1. Listen to yourself, meditate, and pray to discover what your basic needs are, and what direction you want to go.

2. Define those needs operationally: what must be done to meet them, how to do what must be done, and how they fit in with life goals.

3. Begin to translate problems into observable, measurable *goals*. Specify what you really want and need to do.

4. Set up a priority system for your goals. Which is the most important? Which must be achieved before you move on to others?

5. Set up realistic means of meeting those goals. This may mean dividing broad goals into categories, so that each step can be accomplished separately.

6. Be ready to change your plan of action if necessary. Evaluate your progress regularly. If you are not making progress, see if the execution of the plan or the plan itself is at fault.

7. Take responsibility for yourself. An encourager can only support you and help evaluate your progress; he can't make changes for you.
8. Transfer what you learn to every area of life, as appropriate.
9. Evaluate your progress with one or two close friends, and see what needs to be done to further your accomplishments and applications.

The next time I saw her, Flo was excited. I could tell by her face, her posture, and her walk that something had happened. "That self-talk we started last week sure makes a difference. I practiced weakening one negative and irrational idea for ten minutes a day, and, do you know, that changed other ideas as well? I feel that I can do more about controlling my thoughts now. I feel more confident, and I believe that God can truly use me as never before. The plan of action has helped me be more consistent. Thanks for all of your help."

Flo is but one example of how someone can be helped by an effective encourager who motivates action. Each contact we have with others can become healing and helpful if we are open to heed the Spirit of God in our relationships.

There is no substitute for hard work in preparing to be an encourager. Each of us must learn to make the most of every opportunity to be of help. We need to develop sensitivity to others' needs. We need to learn how to help spontaneously, and naturally.

Margaret, whose story appeared at the beginning of this book, is an example for each of us. As she said, "The hardest thing for me to bear is that if I had known then what I know now, I think I could have reached that boy."

Prepare now for the unknown opportunities for the future. What do you need to learn to be able to encourage those whom you recognize with needs? What can you do to develop sensitivity to those whose needs you might not recognize?

The principles reviewed for you in this book can help you become an *encourager*, just as Barnabas was (Acts 15:36-39). Even though Mark had failed, Barnabas continued the relationship. Eventually Mark became a leader in the church— no doubt aided by Barnabas' encouragement.

How many Marks do you know? Can you reach out and encourage them? If you allow these principles of encouragement to become tools of the Holy Spirit, God can use you in ways you may never have realized.

With that prayer, this book is written and made available for you. May it help you become a true *Encourager*.

Beware of Stereotypes

Expectations

"Aren't you going to pray before we start counseling?"
"You don't look like a counselor. The pictures I have seen show a man with a beard and a white coat. What is this?"

Many people come to counseling with certain expectations about the helper or the process. They are sometimes bewildered, distrustful, or angry when those expectations are not fulfilled.

Joe had seen TV shows and had read some books on psychology. He thought he knew what should be done. When counseling didn't go the way he had expected, he was upset and disappointed. He felt he wasn't being helped as effectively as he could be.

Dealing with thwarted expectations can become the springboard for the initial development of communication and understanding. Be open to and accepting of the seeker's questions or expressions of disappointment. They indicate his insecurity. He wants to be on familiar territory, not fighting the battle on a foreign field. He is looking for simple things that fit in with his expectations to confirm his belief that he is in the right place, getting the right treatment. When he doesn't find them, he may become resistant. Your task is to help him feel comfortable even in the absence of what he is looking for.

As a lay helper, you may not meet the seeker's expectation of a beard and white coat. Therefore it is imperative to bring his disappointments into the open and to clarify your function early in the contact. In doing this, you provide structure to the counseling situation.

Structuring is an important part of the healing relationship. When we read of Jesus' counseling and ministry, we find he didn't fit people's stereotypes and expectations. As a result his followers were jolted into adopting a new perspective, and they were stimulated to grow.

Often a seeker's expectations indicate areas of difficulty that need exploration. For example, wanting prayer before, during or after sessions may indicate that he wants divine intervention rather than having to work on the problem himself. If you conform to his expectation, you will fall into the trap that perpetuates his problems. You must resist the trap and clarify to him what you believe effective counseling to entail. In addition, you might note that never in the recorded history of Jesus' contacts did he pray with a person who came to him for help.

If your seeker comes to you thinking that his problems are a punishment from God rather than a result of his personal maladjustment, he may want prayer for forgiveness, and expect you to be the instrument by which God will forgive. Such a prayer may be necessary, but only as a first step. It is not the panacea that will make make everything magically right. The next step requires work on his poor adjustment and poor interpersonal relationships.

These warnings are not to imply that you should never pray with a seeker or conform to any of his expectations.

Just be sure that you know the reasons behind his expectations and requests.

The hymn writer had it right. God has not promised easy solutions, but he has promised strength for the day. The prayer for strength is a healthy prayer. The prayer for escape or for sudden healing could be avoidance or it could be a valid petition. Helping your seeker discover his true motivation will encourage growth. As you carefully guide him, your seeker will gradually learn to be more realistic about the ways that the Spirit of God can use you to help him.

Wanting a Diagnosis

"What is the name for the problem I have? My friends ask me why I'm being counseled, and I want to give them a name. If I don't have a label for my problems, how can I work on them?"

Sam wanted a name for his difficulty. But labeling is usually not helpful, because naming the problem is often taken as a prescription for a plan of action. Each person is unique, and individualized plans of action must be developed for each one. Otherwise, computers or books with complete lists of problems and solutions, rather than another person, could be consulted.

Because a diagnosis is not necessary, you as facilitator need not feel that you must be able to formulate one in order to be helpful. Anyone can be encouraging and healing in a relationship if he is using the proper skills.

Feeling Worse Before Feeling Better

Mary was frustrated. She had met with her encourager over coffee, in her home, in an office, or at church for several weeks. Sometimes she felt that the more she talked, the more confused she became, although it felt good to be able to express her thoughts.

Often in talking with her encourager, she had relived unpleasant experiences from the past, and many of her original negative emotions had come flooding back. She wondered, *Is it really worth it to go over all those things? I seem to get worse instead of better. It takes me a couple days to recover from those sessions! This introspection doesn't seem to be helping anything.*

Sometimes the process of encouraging does seem to be hurting rather that helping. We must be willing to acknowledge that. Deciding how to act on painful insights can help alleviate some of the pain. You can also encourage the seeker by reminding him, "Each time you review the negative past, you will get a more realistic perspective on it, and each time it will feel less painful than it did before."

In recreating the past in memory, finding reasons for negative feelings lessens their effect. Dealing with those feelings lets the seeker move on to deal with current matters more effectively because he is able to let go of more and more of the negative baggage of the past. Reminding your seeker of that fact may be necessary at times, especially when he feels low during or after a session. As he grows, his depression will probably pass quickly. (If it continues over a long period of time or begins interfering with his day-to-day functioning, it would be wise to consider referring him to a Christian professional.)

Communication Gaps

Even though you reflect feelings and are attending well, there may be gaps in communication. For example, your response to a person may not match what he has said. Progress in building your relationship will be delayed until the misunderstanding is cleared up.

Other times a double message may be the cause of the problem. His words are, "I'm calm," but his body message is, "I'm nervous, upset." In such cases, you must communicate what appears to be the true message in your response. Don't be afraid of being wrong; the person will correct you if you are.

Sometimes your own distortion causes problems in communicating. All the information that comes to you is filtered through your own frame of reference. If you have prejudices or negative feelings of which you are unaware, your response will probably cloud the communication rather than clarify it. This is especially important to note in cross-cultural communication.

Another communication gap may result from a fear that the seeker will take advantage of you, which causes you to respond differently than you would if you were not afraid.

To communicate effectively, you must be at least minimally aware of your own feelings, especially those which have been aroused by another person's story. You must also be aware of his true feelings so that you can respond to them accurately. Most gaps in communication are bridged when you are clear about your own and the other's feelings and are able to respond with genuineness and understanding.

Silence

Even when you are non judgmental, most people tend to become silent after they have revealed something deep and significant. In the initial stage of developing rapport, most facilitators find this silence difficult to deal with. But if you take responsibility for keeping the conversation going, the value of silence will be reduced.

In order to build a caring relationship, you must discover the significance of silence. Questioning or trying to keep things moving will prevent you from finding out what the silence means. Instead, relax and wait.

Sometimes silence means that the person is resisting you. You may have said something that he has misinterpreted. Or perhaps he doesn't trust you enough to engage in further exploration. In addition to silence, he may indicate a problem in the relationship by looking around awkwardly, flushing, or changing the subject abruptly, seemingly without good reason.

Silence can become a context in which to discuss the here and now. Helping another explore his reticence provides an opportunity for both of you to learn how to deal with an immediate problem in relationship.

Sometimes silence means that the individual is letting new ideas sink in. Perhaps he is pondering how the different subjects he has discussed can fit together in a new way. He may be organizing his thoughts before saying something new. He may be hurting; going too fast worsens his pain and he wants to gain strength before going on. Those are "good" silences, which should not be interrupted.

The problem, of course, is how to tell whether a silence is valuable or not. If there is an absence of the negative signs noted above, the seeker's silence probably should not be interrupted. You might simply say, "It's good to quietly think, isn't it?" Then if a problem is causing the silence, he can easily tell you so. But if it is a good silence, he can affirm your statement and remain silent. As you sit quietly with him, you may learn more about him.

Defining Responsibility

In helping another, you must maintain a careful balance between true encouragement and helping too much. Too much help from the facilitatior leads to unplanned dependence; too little may turn him away.

The amount and kind of assistance you give should be defined by the seeker. Helping another without his request or consent is demeaning; it may damage his self-image and self-esteem. Instead of helping, you may in fact be hindering him. You must help him accept his own responsibility for feelings and actions.

From the outset, make your expectations regarding responsibility clear to the one you are helping. Carefully spell out your limits. The amount of responsibility you should take varies with the nature of the crisis and the needs of the seeker. At the beginning of the relationship you will need to assume more responsibility. Later, your seeker should begin to take more responsibility, until he reaches the point where he no longer needs your help. Once you have agreed to help, work to make the relationship productive until the other withdraws from the relationship, whether because his needs have been met or because he has decided to relate to someone else.

When you have helped someone—your child, a friend, or one with special problems—to outgrow his need for you, you may find yourself feeling rejected. However, it is at that point that you can enjoy a truly rich, reciprocal relationship with him. You can be pleased that you have helped him become independent.

John the Baptist may have felt rejected when his own disciples left him to follow Jesus (John 1:27). But with the sorrow, he must also have felt joy in having accomplished his purpose.

Keep Alert
To All Resources

From time to time people will come to you whose problems are beyond your ability to help. It is essential that you recognize your own limitations and not try to handle a case that really needs professional attention. To continue to work with a person when you are beyond your depth will ultimately do more harm than good. The truly caring thing to do, in some cases, is to refer a seeker to someone who is especially equipped to deal with his problems.

When Is a Professional Needed?

It is always helpful to have a professional with whom you can talk over your problem cases in informal consultation. At times, however, you will need not only to consult with a professional but to refer cases to him. Referral to a professional should be considered in the following situations:

1. If after an extended time in the relationship the seeker feels worse or seems to be having more severe problems in living, you should refer him to a professional. Early in the relationship, as a person reviews a lot of negative

material in a short space of time, feeling less well is to be expected. But the feelings thus engendered should be only temporary.

2. If physical symptoms continue or get worse, a complete physical examination is in order. Psychological and physical symptoms are often correlated, and the effects of physical ailments often are reduced through talking therapy. An actual physical illness, however, requires medical treatment, and to delay physical care will be detrimental.

3. If a person is in a deep depression that lasts a long time and does not lift with a change in circumstances or with continued support, you should refer him to a professional. Most depressions are situational—a relatively normal response to problems—and the mood can change quickly. But when depression lasts for months, it's time to refer.

4. If a person experiences extremely high moods followed by low ones, consider referring him. Often a shift to a happier mood is interpreted as progress. But if his "high" is more extreme than seems appropriate, and he starts talking about doing unrealistic things, referral may be necessary. If over a long period of time the person alternates between highs and lows, he definitely needs professional attention.

5. If a person begins to make concrete plans for suicide, referral to a Christian professional is crucial. Probe to discover how seriously and concretely he is thinking about suicide. Casual talk or thoughts about suicide may not be significant; most of us, at one time or another, have thought life was too difficult to live. However, if the person makes suicidal plans or asks questions such as, "How many pills will it take to kill a person?" quick referral is essential.

6. If the person is making serious plans to harm another

person, you must refer. Most states have laws that require you, if you have such information, to report it to the threatened person. Not to do so will make you liable for prosecution. If you can convince the person to inform the threatened person himself, do so. But referral to a professional is necessary in any case.

7. If a person is abusing a child, you must refer him to a professional. In some states, you are required also to report such abuse to the police or to a child-protection agency, especially if he is sexually exploiting the child. If possible, convince the person to turn himself in to the authorities to get necessary help.

8. If a person has extremely violent outbursts of anger during which he hurts others, especially a spouse, such evidence of total loss of control should prompt you to refer him to a professional who can give him more in-depth psychotherapy.

9. If a person seems to be losing contact with the real world, refer. Fleeting irrational thoughts are not uncommon as a person works on his problems with an encourager. Expressing irrational thoughts is often enough to help him see their folly. However, if most of what he says over a period of time is irrational, and he does not seem to realize it, he needs professional help.

10. Similarly, if a person retreats into a dream world each time he faces a problem or wants to avoid a conflict, he probably needs to see a professional. Fantasy can enrich life, but if it takes over as a way of dealing with problems and the person does not respond to your encouragement to act realistically on his difficulties, refer.

11. If a person has a serious phobia—an irrational and debilitating fear of something, someone, or some place—you should refer him. Fears are important in helping us learn how to adjust realistically to life, but when fear begins to take a major role, changing previously con-

structive behavior into nonproductive behavior, professional help is needed.

12. If you just don't get along with a person who comes to you for help, refer him to someone else. Each of us is unique; sometimes our own idiosyncrasies are incompatible with those of the seeker, and the kind of close relationship required for encouragement is impossible. A different encourager may be all that is needed. However, if the seeker's interpersonal problems seem to be serious, a professional may be the one to help.

13. If a person demands too much time from you, it may be that he has developed too great a dependency on you, which needs to be adjusted. If you find changing that dependency difficult, or if the person resists changing it, referral to another facilitator may be the most helpful thing you can do for him. If he is deeply dependent, a professional may be necessary.

To Whom Should I Refer?

There are several ways to find referral sources.

1. Ask your pastor whom he refers people to. Follow up on his recommendations, however, and get to know the referral sources he recommends so that you will know whether an individual will be appropriate for your seeker.

2. The Christian Association for Psychological Studies (CAPS), 26705 Farmington Road, Farmington Hills, MI 48018 (Phone 313/477-1350), has a nationwide directory of Christian counselors who can be investigated for their suitability to your seeker's needs. The western region of CAPS also has a directory.

3. Your medical doctor may have information about good referral sources.

4. If all else fails, you may want to check the yellow

pages in the phone book. However, you must carefully screen practitioners listed there to be sure of their competence and philosophy. Merely asking whether they are Christian or where they went to school is not enough.

How Should I Refer?

You have established a warm relationship with another person, but now you feel he needs more help than you can give. Breaking that intimate relationship will be hard to do, but it is necessary.

Be honest. Tell your seeker that the time and expertise he needs go beyond your capability. Assure him that referring doesn't necessarily mean you will pull out of your relationship with him completely. You may be able to team up with the professional; at least you can cooperate with the professional in your encouraging relationship.

Be confident about your referral source, and communicate that confidence to your friend. (Talk to the professional ahead of time to find out what his philosophy of life is. If he is not a Christian, much of the help you have given may be misunderstood. Find out if he is willing to work with you in helping your seeker. If he is not, he probably is not a good referral source.)

When you have found someone in whom you have confidence, discuss the case with him (having first obtained the seeker's *written* permission). Help him to become familiar with the problem as you see it. Then reassure your seeker that you have prepared the way.

Encourage your seeker to explore with you his feelings about being referred to another. Referral is often interpreted as rejection. Emphasize that rather than rejection, the referral is an act of concern and love. This procedure can disarm many negative feelings he may have about the referral.

Additional Reading

By now you have learned that you can be encouraging, therapeutic and healing in your relationships with others. I hope you will expand your interest and understanding by reading other books and manuals about therapeutic relationships.

Be careful, however, in choosing what you read. It's best to avoid books on "counseling" by preachers or seminary professors who aren't psychologists. They often contain half-truths or over-generalizations that can create problems. Use the Scriptures to assess the value of books on "Biblical therapy" or "Biblical psychology." Many are not as Biblical as they purport to be. Therefore, be careful in recommending them to people you are helping.

Likewise, use the truths of Scripture to evaluate the theories and techniques of non-Christian helpers. Where it is true, psychology can be integrated successfully with Biblical truth. But don't allow psychological theories to negate the Biblical truths you already know.

Following are some books you might find helpful as you continue in your endeavors to be an encourager. Not all of them are by Christian authors, but all contain truths that can be used effectively by the Christian encourager working through the power of the Holy Spirit.

Backus, W. & M. Chapian, *Telling Yourself the Truth*. Minneapolis: Bethany, 1980.
This book applies the principles of dealing with depressive thoughts by changing the thinking processes through constructive Christian thinking.

Beck, Aaron et al, *Cognitive Therapy of Depression*. N.Y. Guilford. 425 p. 1979.
A rather comprehensive and complicated resource book on be-

havior and thought process treatment of depression. Many ideas are useful to understand and treat persons. Specific procedures and forms to use are included from a secular frame of reference.

Corey, Gerald, *Case Approach to Counseling and Psychotherapy.* Monterey: Brooks/Cole 131 pp. 1982.
This book gives examples of 8 different styles of counseling, including the major methods and philosophy. Cases are used to illustrate procedures and give a practical understanding of secular approaches.

Corey, G., *I Never Knew I Had A Choice* (2nd edition). Monterey: Brooks/Cole. 1982.
A simple book outlining the personal responsibility of the individual in our society from a non-Christian point of view. You may not agree with all the ideas presented, but the concepts are stimulating and require thought. Exercises and study guides are helpful.

Egan, G., *The Skilled Helper* (2nd edition). Monterey: Brooks/Cole 1982.
An excellent book on practical methods relating to your client. The book covers many areas of helping, and is a good reference book from a secular viewpoint.

Friesen, Gary, *Decision Making and the Will of God.* Portland: Multnomah. 1982.
A source book that can help you in your own life concerning God's will, but especially as you help others. This is an unusual but stimulating approach to important areas of life much needed as a basis for counseling.

Johnson, David W., *Reaching Out.* N.J.: Prentice Hall, 308 p. 1981.
An excellent book with many exercises for developing interpersonal effectiveness and self actualization. Especially good section on handling conflicts and stress from a secular viewpoint.

Lindquist, Stanley, *Christian Psychology,* in Beebe, Ed. *"The Encounter Between Science and Christianity."* Baker, 1965.
This chapter gives the underpinning of Christian faith and psychology as an introduction and foundation to psychotherapy.

Other chapters discuss the relationship of other disciplines also.

Lindquist, Stanley, *Action Helping Skills*. Fresno: Link Care Press, 1976.
A skill book listing specific methods for developing relationships and dissolving barriers in the communication process.

Powell, John, *Why Am I Afraid To Tell You Who I Am?* Niles, Ill: Argus 1969.

Roe, John, *A Consumers Guide to Christian Counseling*. Nashville: Abingdon. 143pp. 1982.
A general information book about procedures, sources and definitions of counseling from a Christian point of view. Topics like problems, counseling process, costs and glossary of terms are included.

ADDENDUM

How to Communicate Cross Culturally

The basic principles presented here are in one sense supra-cultural to a degree. Each concept deals with human nature, and the basic feelings, drives, needs and desires of man are common to all cultures. Therefore anytime we address those basic needs, we are dealing with cross-cultural factors.

The problem we all have is one of encoding-translating-the concepts into acceptable and understandable words, gestures, and non-verbal components so that the person receiving the message truly understands. Whatever the message, it has to be heard and received before it will have any effect on the person accepting the communication. One can verbalize indefinitely to a person, but if they don't understand, our words are of little value.

The over-riding challenge to each one of us boils down to the basic principle of, "What do I know about this person that will allow me to translate my words into a message that is understandable and acceptable to him so that what I say will make an impression?" The principles of genuineness, concern, acceptance and desire to communicate are common to most cultures. The way they are encoded-expressed-may be quite different. Our responsibility is to take these principles, translate them into understandable techniques, so we can communicate the message of the love of God to all those we contact. This then becomes the primary opportunity for each of us to be the true servant of God, glorifying Him in all aspects of our life.   Stanley E. Lindquist, Ph.D.